INSPIRE!

Women's Stories of Accomplishment, Encouragement and Influence

Get ready to be inspired! This book is full of honest and moving stories that will help women realize that no matter what stage of life you're in, you're not alone.

- Kasey Arena, Certified Personal Trainer and Blogger at Powercakes.net

The wonderful stories in this book are a must read for every woman who wants to be energized, renewed and inspired to move in a positive direction to becoming all she can be.

- Donna Stewart, Entrepreneur, Blogger at DonnaStewartOnline.com and Founder of DebtFreeIsSexy.com

In this inspiring book you will find powerful and heartfelt stories of empowerment; it delivers the kind of impact that will enable you to start changing your life's trajectory right this minute.

- Robin Hallett, Intuitive Healer, Founder of RobinHallett.com

Women who read this book are going to be inspired and challenged to become the woman they always dreamed of being. The stories of these 25 women will motivate each of us to think outside the box and to realize that we can attempt great things we never thought possible. I loved this book and each of the heartwarming stories of these phenomenal women.

- Carole Lewis, First Place 4 Health Director Emeritus and author of *Live Life Right Here Right Now*

I truly admire women who have the courage to document their fears and lessons learned, especially in an environment today that is not always friendly or receptive to intellectual honesty and truth. These magnificent women made a bold declaration to write and acknowledge some of their most INSPIRING learning moments, times where they had to wrestle with issues such as personal value and worth in business and in life.

- Patty Azar, Chief Strategy Officer, Vision Alignment, Inc., Creator of Breaking The Good Girl Syndrome®

Often women feel like they have no choice but to become victims of their circumstances. As the title promises, you'll find inspiration from these 25 women and learn ways to approach adversity with an optimistic and life-changing perspective.

- **Laurie Itkin,** Financial Advisor and author of *Every Woman Should Know Her Options*

Compelling. Real. Heart-felt. Inspiring. These powerful essays are emblazoned with the physical and emotional challenges, conflicts, fears and victories that embody what it is to be "woman."

- **Debra Boulanger,** Founder of Live a Whole Life and Creator of The Great Do-Over – Life and Love After Divorce

Sometimes it takes a while for something to arouse our inner faculties and influence us to achieve greater heights. INSPIRE has that rare ability to help us reach for what we know is possible.

- **Jeni Scott,** Author, Owner and Creative Mind at Bakerette.com

INSPIRE is a powerful anthology of inspirational stories shared by amazing women who have found their path to success. It is a must read for all who dream of making a difference.

- **Lillie Leonardi,** Author of *In The Shadow Of A Badge: A Memoir About Flight 93, A Field Of Angels* (Hay House Publishing)

Real People, Real Inspiration, a Real Good Read!! In your business or in the business of living, we all help each other by sharing real life stories of strength and encouragement. These stories refresh my soul, and I know they will renew yours too!

- **Deb Scott,** Award Winning Author: *The Sky is Green & The Grass is Blue* (a Top 20 Kindle BestSeller), Award Winning Podcaster, The Best People We Know Show with over 1 Million Global Listeners. GreenSkyAndBlueGrass.com

Dedication

To women everywhere whose accomplishments will influence others and make a difference in the world.

Contents

Beth Caldwell

"*Reflect on your priorities and don't be afraid to readjust.*"
- Brian Nuckols

Chapter One:

YES, YOU CAN DO IT ALL...
JUST NOT AT THE SAME TIME

I had just received the job offer of my dreams. I could hardly believe it. An up-and-coming company offered me a position teaching workshops to their staff of more than 1,200 teachers, social workers and daycare providers. The job paid close to six figures, had great benefits and lots of VIP perks. As a single mom, it represented my key to independence; I'd no longer have to rely on my ex-husband to help make ends meet each month. I would be able to move my sons into a beautiful home in the suburbs and send them to a better school. My car at the time was so old and beat up that I had to carry oil and water in the trunk at all times. My two boys knew that whenever smoke began to seep out from under the hood they were to alert me so that I could refill whatever fluid was running low. I couldn't wait to buy a new car and I was already picturing the vacations that we'd finally be able to afford.

This job was absolutely ideal for me and the company's values were very much in alignment with my own. I'd be teaching motivational and inspirational workshops to teachers, helping executives become better leaders, and instructing daycare providers on important childcare

concepts. The owners were passionate about impacting low-income families and innovative in their policies for integrating children with disabilities into all classrooms. The position required three weeks of travel each month - that's three weeks a month making a difference by doing something worthwhile that I loved while earning a great paycheck. There was only one problem and it was an important one: it meant that roughly 75 percent of my time would be away from my boys. At this point, they were six and seven years old. When I realized that the job required this much travel I knew instantly that it was not possible for me to accept it.

My priorities were clear but that doesn't mean I didn't struggle with the decision. I yearned for financial independence. I desperately wanted to give my sons a better education and pay for the expensive sports lessons that their friends enjoyed. So I tried to think of a way to make this new job position fit around my lifestyle. Hiring a full-time nanny could be an option, which I would be able to afford with this salary. Still, I knew in my heart that this arrangement would never work, not for me.

You see, I absolutely loved being a mom. Of all the different roles I've had over the years, being with my boys when they were young was my most favorite. I truly enjoyed them and was most happy when I was doing things with them. I had an excellent part-time job that offered me a lot of flexibility. We were very active at our church, their school and in our community; other than not being in a more comfortable financial position, I was very happy with my life just as it was.

Still, I imagined how our lives would be changed with the financial security that this position offered, and I felt torn. Would I be any happier if my bank account had a few extra zeroes? Part of me believed that filling that "missing piece" would complete my life, yet I knew it would not be the right

decision for us as a family. After a week of obsessing about this choice I called the owners of the company and let them know my decision. I earnestly asked them to reconsider me for any position that did not include as much travel. They couldn't understand how anyone could walk away from such a great opportunity. They were shocked and perplexed.

I felt confident about my decision. I knew I made the right choice, but was also very disappointed and upset about it for several weeks. I remember thinking that I would never, ever get another opportunity to work in a job that I loved so much and paid so well. I felt extremely guilty for walking away from an opportunity to give my sons a better life. Even though weeks had passed since I'd declined the position, I still thought about it every day. One afternoon as I was at my kitchen table writing out checks to pay bills, I looked at my bank balance and thought, If you had taken that job, you could have it all.

**Of all the jobs I've had, being with my boys
when they were young was my favorite.**

Immediately, my inner voice replied, *You DO have it all. You have a nice home and healthy, happy children. You work flexible hours, have enough money to cover your expenses*

and you get to spend all the time you want with your children. You already have it all. Lots of women would give up their paychecks to enjoy what you have. This isn't the last job you'll ever be offered. In 10 years you'll be able to travel and something even better will happen for you. Yes, you CAN have it all; you just can't have it all at the same time.

This message was powerful. I felt that God had spoken directly to me. From that moment on, I stopped feeling guilty about declining the job offer. Instead, I began to acknowledge the many blessings in my life. I didn't have financial independence yet but I was independent. Just six months later, that company went bankrupt; 1,200 employees in three states went to work one morning and found the doors locked with a sign: "Out of Business." When I heard this news, my heart broke for everyone who had lost their job. In the same breath, a wave of peace washed over me. I had listened to my inner voice and it didn't steer me wrong.

Over the next several years, I continued to do what I loved best: being a mom. I worked part time and pursued my passion of writing and speaking to motivate women in whatever spare time I could find. Occasionally, I'd feel a twinge of guilt that my boys weren't in the best schools or weren't playing on exclusive traveling sports teams. We spent our summers at the public pool while our friends traveled to the beach or Walt Disney World. At times, I felt envious but then I'd remember that powerful message: *You can have it all, just not all at the same time.* This brought me peace and kept me feeling content with my present life and curious about my future.

Over the years, I've built my own empire and developed creative ways to earn money while keeping my priorities in order. Even though my boys are grown now, I still want to be available when they call, visit or need to talk. Owning my

own business gives me control over my schedule and allows me to spend time with the people who are most important to me. I can work odd hours if I want (my clients are very familiar with my late night emails!) and I get to take advantage of my creativity whenever the muse strikes. I have developed a large network of women who support one another. I've written several books and created dozens of workshops and programs that help other women succeed in life and business. My work takes me around the world, where I meet and interact with women in all stages of life. I wonder where I would be today if I had ignored that little voice in my head many years ago.

> *"Things will never again be
> as they are today.
> Do what's best for you right now."*

Today, when I talk with women, they often share their frustrations about work and family. They feel guilty, worried and even resentful about the demands on their time. They feel like they are part of a big rat race, and overwhelmed with the expectations they place on themselves. Many struggle financially while trying to keep up with their neighbors. Trying to accomplish everything at once is a disservice to the entire family, especially when everyone is frustrated, struggling and upset. Remember, rat races are for rats, not human beings.

Sometimes we get so busy doing everything that we think we're supposed to do that we forget why we're doing it in the first place. I know for sure that we're not supposed to live our lives feeling upset, guilty, overwhelmed and worried all the time.

If this describes you, please stop. Take some time right now

and think about what is really important at this point in your life. Listen to your inner voice; it won't lie to you. If it's your career, put your focus there and don't feel guilty. If right now is the time that should be dedicated to your family, go fully into it and don't spend a moment wondering what others might think. The only opinions that really matter are the ones of those closest and most important to you - and only if they truly have your best interest at heart. Remember that life changes. Things will never again be as they are today. What's important today will be different in 10 years or so. Do what is best for you and your loved ones right now. You'll never get this time back.

Recently, I had an impressive job offer from a prestigious company, much like the one I stressed over all those years ago: six-figure salary, expense account and other perks, a full support team. Along with all of that came travel, long hours and the corporate grind. This time, I took a matter of minutes to make my decision. "I'll think about it . . . in about 10 years," I told them.

Beth Caldwell is a popular author and business strategist who helps her clients succeed in life and business. She's best known as the founder of her organization Pittsburgh Professional Women. In 2013, Beth became a contributing writer for the Pittsburgh Business Times, launched Leadership Academy for Women and wrote her newest book, "Smart Leadership: 12 Simple Strategies to Help You Shift from Ineffective Boss to Brilliant Leader." Her other books include "I Wish I'd Known THAT, Secrets to Success in Business" and "Empower: Stories of Breakthrough, Triumph and Discovery." Beth is a "40 Under 40" award winner, having been recognized by Pittsburgh Magazine as one of the city's most influential young leaders. Learn more at Beth-Caldwell.com.

Lisa Hamer Jenkins

"Nobody can go back and start a new beginning, but anyone can start today and make a new ending."

\- Marie Robinson

Chapter Two

MOM WENT RUNNING

Overwhelmed. Overworked. Overweight. Only 37 years old. Caregiving spouse to a former pastor. Raising two young children. Working full-time as a social worker specializing in dementia care.

My personal and work lives were filled with serving others. As a professional caregiver, I was aware of the need to be healthy and well rested, yet I could not seem to get this under control in my personal life. My stress level was high, as were my weight and blood pressure. I was constantly in desperate need of a good night's sleep. During my times of deepest exhaustion, I clung to Galatians 6:9: *Let us not become weary in doing good, for at the proper time we will reap a harvest if we do not give up.* I was determined not to give up but was growing weary... very weary. Where was the harvest?

One November night while my family slept and I was still doing housework at 11:00 p.m., I was overtaken with frustration, sadness and anger. It seemed that I couldn't endure another moment of giving and giving and giving. I was emotionally, spiritually and physically exhausted. Almost involuntarily, I walked out the front door. No coat. No keys.

No phone. No note. I stepped outside onto the pavement and went running. Literally.

Sadly, no one sent out a search party. In fact, no one even noticed that I was gone. I circled the block and then returned. Even after that short trip, I noticed that my chest felt lighter. My head was clearer. My shoulders more relaxed. I felt pretty good. So I went around the block the next night and the next and so on. One night while walking, I reflected on the Bible verse that I held so close and realized that I was so focused on doing good for everyone else that I was ignoring one key person: me! Walking that short loop became my daily time of doing something good for me.

Part of my job at that time was to teach wellness classes for older adults at an adult day health center. In one class, we discussed taking small steps toward larger goals. After finishing the class, I sat at my desk feeling very conflicted. Here I was encouraging people in their 80's to never stop setting goals, to step out of their comfort zones and try something new; meanwhile, I was frozen in a very unhappy and unhealthy place. I felt like a phony.

With a deep sigh I turned my desk chair to check my email. In my in-box was an unsolicited message from a large wellness company. Normally, I would automatically hit delete but the headline on this one caught my eye. "From Sofa Slug to 5K Star in 15 Weeks." Even though I knew that message had been sent to thousands of people, I felt like it was directed solely at me. *A couch to 5k training program?* I leaned back in my chair and stared at the screen. *Running a 5K. Could I run for 3.1 miles?* I had seen pictures of my sister and brother-in-law at a few 5K races. *They looked like they were having fun, and 3.1 miles isn't that far of a distance. Is this something I could do?* The last time I remembered running was in gym class during my senior year of high

school. I didn't enjoy it. Now, I couldn't even walk around my block without my chest heaving and my legs burning. It was crazy to even consider running.

That night my mind kept returning to the email. By this time I had been taking my routine walk for almost a month. While I was feeling better physically, I was literally walking in circles with no destination or goal. *When was the last time I had set a goal for myself?* I couldn't even remember. *When was the last time I tried something new?* I had no idea. *Could I possibly run for 3.1 miles?* I began to feel a sense of excitement well up in my gut. *Why not set that "couch to 5k" goal?* I made up my mind to do it. I was going to train for and actually run a 5K race.

"I told absolutely everyone. I even announced it on Facebook."

I went straight to the computer and pulled up the email, which laid out the 15-week training program. I grabbed my calendar and counted out 15 weeks, which took me to the middle of April. Perfect! There was a 5K race happening in my hometown on April 10. My goal was set: On April 10, 2010, I would complete my first 5K race.

Part of me wanted to keep this a secret. After all, I was a 37-year-old overwhelmed, overworked and overweight caregiver with two children and a full-time job. Achieving this goal didn't seem likely. My thoughts returned to how awful I felt earlier in the day while at my desk - frozen, conflicted, like a phony. Then I felt that twinge of excitement well up again. So I did the opposite: I told absolutely everyone. I even announced it (gulp!) on Facebook.

My late night walks around the block were replaced with a new training regimen. I had been trying for years to fit my life into the exercise class schedule at the gym, arriving late or rushing out early. I'd set my alarm for 5:00 a.m. like several of my friends, only to hit snooze 10 times instead of jumping out of bed and into my walking shoes. I discovered that I needed to stop trying to be like everyone else and exercise on my own schedule. As it turns out, running at 11:00 p.m. is the perfect time for me.

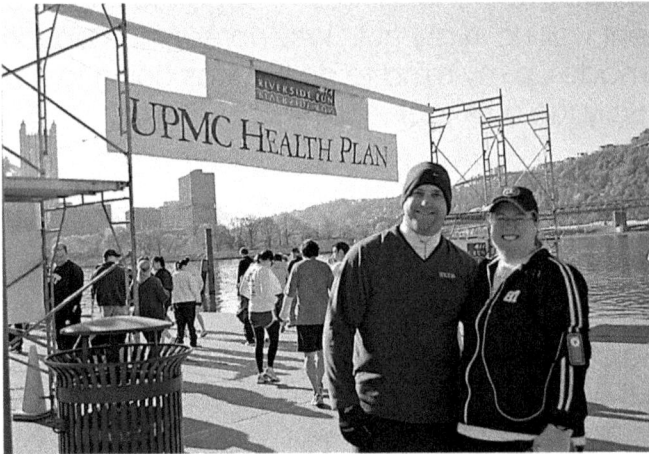

First 5K race with my brother-in-law Chris.

Those 15 weeks flew by, and I followed my training schedule as best as I could. While I hadn't yet ran the full 3.1 miles, I could easily run/walk that distance. I refined my goal to complete the 5K in under 45 minutes, making it across that finish line any way I could.

On the morning of the race, I found myself standing with my brother-in-law Chris, whom I had asked to run with me, in the middle of a crowd at the starting line. My cell phone buzzed continuously with encouraging text messages. My Facebook page was filled with posts from friends around the country

wishing me luck and waiting for results from the big event. I felt excited and terrified at the same time.

As I saw the sun rising, it suddenly dawned on me that this would be my first run in the daylight. No one had ever seen me run, and I always ran alone. As I looked side to side, I couldn't help but notice that I was surrounded by fit, thin people in trendy running gear. I looked down at my double XL sweatpants purchased from a thrift shop and began to feel that I had made a very big mistake.

Feeling like I didn't belong there, I left my place in line and walked over to my sister.

"We have to leave now," I told her in no uncertain terms.

"You are fine," she said with a smile. She put her hands on my shoulders, turned me around and gave me a slight push back into the crowd. I felt sick.

When the starting gun sounded, the sound of hundreds of pairs of running shoes slapping the pavement echoed in my ears. Chris and I started to run. I felt like I was sprinting. People bumped into me from all sides. I became overwhelmed and began to panic. I came to a complete stop and burst into tears. Chris quickly pulled me off to the side.

"What are you doing?" he asked, puzzled.

"I can't do this!" I sobbed. "I'm not ready! I don't know what I was thinking. This is the most stupid idea I've ever had. Let's go! We already have the t-shirt. No one has to know that I didn't finish."

"Look," he said calmly. "This is what we're going to do. We're

going to let everyone run past us. Then we're going to get back on the course and we will run, walk or crawl if we have to until we finish the 3.1 miles. You can do this."

That is exactly what we did. After the crowd passed, I noticed two sets of runners approaching. Each pair had a person who looked just like me: A little overweight. A little nervous. A little out of place. We got back on the course and the six of us completed the 5K together. We ran, we walked and we encouraged each other the whole way.

Chris and I came in next to last among the runners. Our time was 43:16. I had achieved my goal! The runners who had finished ahead of us lined each side of the course cheering us to the end. Although running is a competitive sport, they weren't judging me; they were encouraging me. Crossing that finish line was such a high! I felt like a true champion.

The sense of accomplishment that I felt after crossing that finish line was amazing. I did it! I set a goal and met it. I stepped outside of my comfort zone, pushed aside great fear and did something I had never done before or dreamed I could do. What started out to be scary and overwhelming became one of the most powerful events of my life.

You might think that after this race I would be done with running. I had accomplished what I set out to do. Although I had felt like quitting 45 minutes earlier, the sense of victory at the finish line far outweighed the fear at the start. I continued my nightly runs. Three months later I completed my second 5K race. To date, I've completed 43 races, including three 10k's and an eight-mile event. In celebration of my 40th birthday in 2013, I completed a half-marathon. My ongoing goal is to complete one 5K a month. Since I started running, I'm at a healthier weight, my blood pressure is under control and I have more energy.

I continue to post my goals and runs on Facebook. My accomplishments have become a regular topic of conversation at family and social gatherings. It seems as though I'm always running into someone who has just started their wellness journey. At nearly every race, I end up crossing paths with a rookie runner who needs encouragement. Not long after my first race, I found myself answering dozens of emails a week from people looking for inspiration. It made sense to put all of my information and experiences in one place. In January 2012, I launched www.momwentrunning.com.

Let us not become weary in doing good, for at the proper time we will reap a harvest if we do not give up. I still have that verse posted around my home and office. When I see it, I no longer feel weary; I feel victorious. I didn't give up - not only on that "Sofa Slug to 5K" course but on the life I've been given. Life is not perfect but it is better. Overwhelmed, overworked and overweight has been replaced with a happy and healthy harvest of goodness.

Lisa Hamer Jenkins *is a caregiving spouse, mother of two and a social worker specializing in dementia care. In 2010, she was an overwhelmed, overworked and overweight woman whose life was full of serving others. Determined not to give-up, Lisa decided it was time to regain control of her health. Fifteen weeks later she completed her first 5K. Finishing that race was a pivotal experience in her life. Today, while her life responsibilities have not changed, her perspective has shifted. Lisa shares her journey and provides inspiration to others as a mentor and motivational speaker. Visit her popular blog momwentrunning.com.*

Bebe M. Kinnett

"Do one thing every day that scares you."

\- Eleanor Roosevelt

Chapter Three
THE PILL I WOULDN'T SWALLOW

*W*hile nestled on a cozy picnic blanket at the foot of an historic covered bridge, Jim proudly presented a diamond engagement ring. I squealed with excitement! Slipping it on my finger was one of the best decisions I've ever made. My parent's home provided me with love, warmth and a very happy childhood, but it was time to move on. As I walked down the aisle and my father placed my hand in Jim's, I embarked on a new journey that led us to many new places. Following his career around the country has not only provided wonderful and challenging experiences but has also made us stronger.

When I accepted Jim's marriage proposal, I had no idea that 37 years later we would have torn up roots and lived in eight different places. When we reluctantly moved to enhance Jim's career, he promised me he wouldn't bury me in that river town, and he kept his promise. It was a safe place to raise our three sons, but where did I fit in? Every move provided a challenge on how to use my skills and passions in a new location. After years of working in college career centers, the entrepreneurial spirit sparked inside of me and I created Absolute Web Designs. On the surface,

starting a technology business completely defied logic. Why would a counselor with a bachelor's degree in psychology and master's degree in leadership ever think to open a web design business?

"Why not?" I asked myself. The colleges where I worked had provided exceptional staff training in technology and I seemed to be natural in that kind of work.

Determination can make anything possible. My strong interest in technology, combined with my passion for and dedication to customer service, resulted in the creation of a web design business with a unique philosophy. While similar firms talked "techy" to intimidate their customers, I counseled my clients, translated their needs into understandable visual descriptions then worked with the technicians so they could create my clients' masterpieces. No question was "too stupid" and my customers appreciated my company's caring philosophy.

Life changed after our youngest son graduated from high school and we felt compelled to move closer to family and friends. Newly self-employed, Jim now had the freedom and flexibility to move anywhere. All I needed was my laptop to relocate my web design business. Oddly enough, this time I wanted to move. Was I crazy? I knew very well that transitions cause stress and I was to find that this one had hidden challenges around every corner.

Optimistic that our old house would sell faster if it was empty and in move-in condition, we used our savings to purchase a second home. Although this approach had been successful with previous moves, this time it was disastrous. Shortly after we purchased a second home, the housing market crashed. Suddenly, we found ourselves owning two homes with no hope of selling either one anytime soon. This tremendous financial strain was obviously not part of our long-range plan.

How could this happen?

The reality of the situation finally set in: Owning two homes made it necessary for me to find a full-time job. Fortunately, I quickly landed a great job as a career counselor at a nearby college. I never expected to enjoy the job so much. My experience as a business owner, combined with my career counseling background, provided a refreshing perspective on employment interviews. My students and I watched interview tapes and laughed at the obscure things people said under stress. Laughing and learning were great tools. This interactive approach to job searching and interviewing resulted in skyrocketing student and graduate employment rates. The college staff and co-workers respected each other and it was a friendly place to go each day. I could have worked at that job forever.

In the meantime, I continued to run my web design business every morning, every lunch, every night after dinner and on weekends. I was still passionate about it but obtaining new customers in a different location proved to be an uphill climb. Rising gas prices and the constant travel between our two houses only added to the stress of working full time, even though I enjoyed my job. The wonderful old house that contained delightful memories of Christmas parties, sleepovers and celebrations became a constant burden. I began to wear down.

One day, I received an invitation to apply for an impressive corporate executive position that included a wonderful salary increase along with responsibility and leadership. It appeared to be the solution to our financial woes. I felt guilty for leaving the job I loved and abandoning my friends at the college but I couldn't turn down the salary boost. I knew this new position would be challenging but what I didn't know was that my predecessor only lasted eight months before he quit.

What happened at my first executive meeting blindsided
me when I realized I'd landed in the middle of a difficult
conflict between a volunteer board and the corporation. My
excitement quickly turned to embarrassment, humiliation and
tremendous guilt. Why did I leave a nurturing environment
only to be bullied? Despite the fact that my team and
I constantly walked on eggshells, we achieved all of our
directives and received outside recognition as one of the
"Best in the State." I also received a raise but that didn't
resolve the problems at hand. The battle between the entities
continued to escalate. One year after leaving a job where
I could have gladly stayed until I retired, I was unemployed.
I had jumped ship for a higher salary and it came at a big
price.

In hindsight, I realized that the bully in this organization was the
kind of person who respected no one and enjoyed belittling
others in order to enhance her status. The more incompetent
she made others appear, the more arrogant she became.
No paycheck is worth that kind of stress. The corporation
lost the contract; suddenly, I was over the age of 50 and
searching for work. I was very angry and my confidence was
slowly disintegrating.

After years of helping others write resumes, learn how to
interview and find employment, there I was on the other side
of the desk. In the past, if I was passionate about a position, I
could usually present myself well enough to get hired, so I was
never out of work for long.

Things were different now. For every job I applied for, I was
too old, too experienced, too un-specialized or too costly. I
refused to believe that I was too "whatever" and continued
to submit resumes. Every dreaded rejection letter after an
interview became an insult that chipped away at my self-
esteem. Although I consistently ranked in the top candidates,

the winners were always younger. For the first time in my life, I felt obsolete. I always looked forward to enhancing my career and I couldn't accept that I was "worthless." Gradually, I began to feel hollow, like one of those cactus toys with the pebbles inside. I made noise but no music.

I needed help to pick myself back up so I decided to ask my doctor for an antidepressant. When he handed me the prescription, relief swelled through my body. As I dreamed of getting back to normal, I stopped to read the warning instructions that the doctor had included. They made me question if medication was the best way to deal with the situation; the potential side effects were alarming. I hid the prescription in my desk because I felt ashamed for needing it. As I weighed all the pros and cons, I discovered that I alone had the power to decide and control my future. Medication wasn't my solution; regaining control of my life was the key to solving my problems.

"It felt so good to tear up that prescription."

Instead of swallowing a pill, I had to begin by making some changes. I decided to revive my web design business, which had been on autopilot. Although my current customers were given red carpet service, there had been little attention to marketing or enhancing these services. Rather than waiting around for someone to discover my potential and hire me, I decided to become my own boss again. Absolute Web Designs was built on trust and respect, and that foundation still existed. My lack of confidence was the only thing holding me back this time.

"Go for it, Bebe!" Jim said with encouragement. I took his advice. It felt so good to reach in the desk drawer and tear

up that prescription.

I joined networking groups and began to spread the word about my passion for customer service and providing a quality product. My background as a counselor helped to establish a trusting relationship with my customers and colleagues. After experiencing bullying in the workplace, I vowed to always treat people with respect and honesty. I didn't want anyone - customers or employees - to suffer through the same belittling experiences I'd had. Gradually, referrals started coming in and the business expanded across the United States.

Women in Business Champion Award, 2013

Establishing business relationships became so important to me that I became president of the Bright Area Business Association. Since then our membership has doubled. Working together, we built a stronger business community. As a result of supporting others, I received the LEADS Women in Business Champion Award in Southeast Indiana. Today I enjoy

networking with other business leaders across the country. Their positive influence energizes and empowers me.

The life of an entrepreneur definitely has its rewards. Despite the ups and downs, I'm grateful that I regained my strength and determination the day I decided to not swallow those antidepressant pills. I have the flexibility to visit my family and grandchildren whenever I want to because technology makes my business portable. By choice, I am never far from my work but I can be where I want to be and spend quality time with those I love. Much of the time you can find me with my wonderful husband of 37 years while we sit by our pond and relax. I have control over my life and it feels good to smile again.

Bebe Kinnett *is a former college career advisor turned entrepreneur. As the owner of Absolute Web Designs, integrating her counseling skills and business savvy, Bebe creates dynamic websites that work as a successful marketing tool for her clients. She holds a BS degree in Psychology and an MA in Leadership. In 2013 Bebe was recognized with the LEADS Women in Business Champion award honoring entrepreneurs in Southeast Indiana. To learn more about her unique web design solutions, visit absolutewebdesigns.com.*

Janelle Cline

"We all have two choices: we can make a living or we can design a life."

- Jim Rohn

Chapter Four

ENGINEER TO ENTREPRENEUR

*I*f there is one thing that I learned when very young, it's that life is way too short. By the age of 29, I had traveled extensively around the world, enjoyed a successful collegiate basketball career, had a prestigious engineering position and married the man of my dreams. Life was going according to my plan. I had it all and my future looked extremely bright.

Then three major events happened in rapid succession that greatly impacted my life. Weeks after my 30th birthday, I lost my mother suddenly to multiple sclerosis and cancer, while being eight months pregnant with my first child. I soon gave birth to a healthy baby girl. Shortly thereafter a car accident left me with a chronic condition that I will have to deal with for the rest of my life.

When my sweet baby girl, Bailey, was just six weeks old, I remember looking down at her snuggled in my arms and thinking, *I can't imagine going back to work right now. How do working moms do it? She is just so tiny and still very precious.* Fortunately, my husband, Travis, is successful in his career and I was able to take six months off with unpaid

maternity leave. We both knew how special and memorable that time would be; the financial price would be well worth it.

Those six months flew by and before I could blink, the day I dreaded was quickly approaching. It was time to return to work. I'd sit in my office chair thinking about how I missed my morning snuggles. I could almost hear Bailey's giggles as I worked on projects. At the end of each day, I couldn't get home fast enough. Going back to the corporate life was quite a wake-up call, mainly since my unpaid maternity leave left me with zero vacation days. After my car accident, I had to continuously beg for unpaid leave and negotiate make-up hours for the numerous doctors' appointments and sick days I had to take. Forget personal days, which we know every mom needs now and again. It was especially rough over the holidays and long winter, as I was used to taking time off to be with family or go on vacations. Being a new mother made me realize that I didn't like having to answer to a boss and having someone else dictate my time. Coupled with losing my mother, I realized that life is too short and wonderful to waste time doing things you really don't want to be doing, especially when it takes away from family.

Shortly after learning I was pregnant with our second child, I received an intriguing phone call. My mother-in-law, Betsy, was in Texas visiting her sister, who had just started a business with Ambit Energy, a company dealing with the deregulation of electricity and natural gas.

"You have to tell Janelle about this," Betsy told her sister, and they picked up the phone to call me. Betsy knew about my health struggles since the accident, how unhappy I was in my career and how I disliked leaving Bailey in daycare for 10 hours a day. She knew I was looking for something lucrative and this opportunity offered a powerful solution. At first I was skeptical.

"What do you mean I can profit by helping people save money on their energy bills?"

It didn't make sense to me because I didn't understand deregulation. I'm very analytical and even though I knew my aunt had become wildly successful after just one year, I did due diligence on both the company and the industry. In my three months of research, I discovered that the United States government had already deregulated the airlines, railroad and long distance telephone industries. I also learned that electricity and natural gas would be the last and largest major utility in the country to ever deregulate. This process was just beginning.

Once I understood all of this, I couldn't believe a potential business opportunity on this large of a scale even existed. I immediately saw what set Ambit apart from every other opportunity I'd been researching: they offered a service instead of product - not just any service but one that consumers needed. This meant that I could forego much of the sales training required in other industries aimed at getting customers to change their buying habits and make purchases that they may not even need. With Ambit, nothing needed to change for a customer; they could continue to use their utility service in the exact same way they always had. Was it too good to be true? Here was a business in which I could generate true residual income month after month, year after year. It offered the type of earning potential that could create financial freedom and free up my time. Genius! I caught the vision of how big this was going to be and I jumped in. I would work part-time as an independent consultant with Ambit Energy while continuing with my full-time job. It was my solid financial escape plan.

Before long, our family was blessed with another girl, Macy. With the added responsibilities of having a second child,

my health quickly spiraled downhill, as I was still dealing with residual effects from the car accident. Keeping up with a toddler and a baby was physically challenging, especially since Travis worked out of town six days a week at this time. I was able to take another six months of unpaid maternity leave from my engineering job. With my hands full, I literally did nothing with my Ambit business for over a year.

Far too soon, the time came for me to return to work once again. Each day began abruptly with the alarm blaring at 5:30 a.m. Moms know the routine: shower, pick out fashionable business attire (the only "feel good" thing about my day), feed everyone breakfast, drop off the children at day care then endure a 30-minute commute to my tiny cubicle while dreaming of being back at home cradling my kids instead of my coffee. Unmotivated and uninspired, I would grind through another day of stuffy meetings and computer work of performing tedious calculations. Late in the day, my body would start to ache and my symptoms would flare up. Most days, I left the office with a pounding headache.

By the time I walked through my front door, I was already exhausted yet as all career women know, mom duty is just beginning for the evening. I resented that I didn't feel well enough to truly enjoy the time at home with my daughters. Travis was my saving grace. He could always tell when I was having a really bad day and was more than happy to change diapers, shop, cook, bathe the girls, get them ready for bedtime, you name it. What a lifesaver. I admire and appreciate him for being an awesome dad and dedicated husband.

When Travis and I married, we never envisioned having a life filled with challenges; I was an athletic, energetic and independent Alaskan woman. I am sure he didn't plan on

being a caregiver to a fragile wife and having so much responsibility for our two small children. Thank God that Travis was willing to be Mr. Mom for a couple of years while I was on a mission to find answers to recurring medical issues stemming from the accident. I did everything I possibly could to feel better because I couldn't imagine a future filled with chronic pain, headaches, cervicogenic dizziness and exhaustion, not to mention the physical limitations and emotional effects. Aside from Travis, I felt so alone. I missed my mom and needed her comforting words telling me that I would get through this and everything would be alright. The doctors weren't helping; they couldn't find the source of my symptoms. It made me so angry.

> *"The power is in your hands.*
> *Own your outcome."*

"Why me?" is a question I repeatedly asked. I just wasn't "myself" anymore.

It all came to a head one day while at the office. It was a gorgeous sunny day and I wasn't feeling well, so I went home. After grabbing the mail, I found a check from the Ambit business I'd started over a year ago. It was four figures! I remember thinking, *I have not done a thing for over a year and I'm getting this amount? I launched this business so I could free up time for family and my health. Imagine if I really applied myself! I could totally replace my salary.*

An inner spark of hope was ignited. I had two adorable girls but was living with chronic pain, an overwhelmed husband and I hated my job; still, we needed the income. I understood the preciousness of time and I began to envision what my life would look like in five years. If I didn't do

something about my situation, nothing would change. In that moment, I chose to own my outcome and get serious about my Ambit business.

Thirty-five months later on June 1, 2012, I did it! I retired from my career as a professional engineer at age 36. For three years, I consistently worked my business part time. I wanted to transition without sacrificing the lifestyle or income that my husband and I had become accustomed to. I did it!

Today I love that when I wake up in the morning, I get to choose how to spend my day. I can attend every one of my daughters' school functions, enjoy lunches with girlfriends, go to the lake on sunny days, sneak away with my husband and take trips with family. I don't have to choose between being there for my family and having a thriving career. It's a freedom and lifestyle that I want to share with other women who are looking for a professional outlet while raising their families.

My team and I share the dream of entrepreneurship and the possibilities it brings. Many have replaced the income from their full-time jobs and are now free to pursue a lifestyle they never thought possible or experienced in the regular nine-to-five world. The ability to link your income to a commodity is what attracts many savvy women to the Ambit Opportunity.

In my opinion, this business model is the best kept secret around for achieving financial independence. We help people, families and businesses discover how to save money on their energy bills (or potentially earn free energy). *Who doesn't want to share that value?* That's why Ambit Energy is the PERFECT business for women. We just do what we love to do, network, tell people about a good deal, help others and have a lot of fun doing it.

Going for my financial dream has been an amazing journey and one of the most rewarding achievements I've ever accomplished. The personal growth and friendships I've acquired are priceless, and it has made me a better wife, mom, business partner and friend. Financial freedom is far more than financial; it means that I'm a woman who is free to be who I really am. Finally, I've returned to being myself, and that's a reward without equal.

The power is in your hands. Own your outcome.

Fun family times in Alaska.

Janelle Cline *retired from her prestigious career as a professional engineer at age 36. A lifelong Alaskan, Janelle, her husband and their two daughters currently live in the small town of North Pole, Alaska. Frustrated and tired of trading her days for dollars in an unfulfilling career, she engineered her way out of the corporate grind. As a successful entrepreneur and the go-to expert for ambitious individuals who want more out of life and business, Janelle teaches how to* **Own Your Outcome**™*. Learn more at JanelleCline.com.*

Sally Power

"When I stand before God at the end of my life, I would hope that I would not have a single bit of talent left, and could say, 'I used everything you gave me'."

- Erma Bombeck

Chapter Five
WHAT'S NEXT, CINDERELLA?

*L*ike so many female Baby Boomers, I had my sights set on the "picture perfect" plan: meet Prince Charming, get married, have a family and live happily ever after... end of story, cut to the credits. By age 27, I was well on my way. It appeared that I had indeed found the man of my dreams. He was tall, dark, extremely handsome and very CHARMING. Within a year, we married and during the first dozen years of our life together, we had three beautiful children. Sadly, the fairy tale had already started to unravel.

Twenty years after tying the knot, Prince Charming and Cinderella were in a desperate situation - financially, emotionally and even spiritually. Attempts to reconcile the relationship were unsuccessful and Cinderella (that would be ME) found herself in the midst of a divorce, inheriting more than $200,000 of debt. OUCH! That wasn't part of the original script. Between the debt, mounting legal fees and raising our children (one preteen and two teens) with minimal to no child support, I found myself in a downward financial spiral - $300 to $400 short each month on expenses. What was I to do? I felt like a discarded dishrag but I didn't want to model for my kids that when crummy things happen in life, you roll over and die.

It was my 50th birthday. I packed the kids into the car and headed to our local amusement park. Why? Well, to ride the Skycoaster, of course! There we were - my daughter, younger son and I strapped into a huge canvas harness while my older son looked on. The ride hoisted us 200 feet in the air. At the pinnacle, my son pulled the ripcord and - gasp! - we plunged into an adrenaline-charged free fall over the lake. For several *long* minutes, we swung in massive arcs over the water. Yes! I was terrified. Yes! I screamed like a baby. And - most important of all - yes! I'd done something that forced me to fearlessly press through my personal terror. If I could survive that, I reasoned, I could certainly deal with my current life circumstances, as well.

Later that same day, I took another great leap. I purchased a women's resale shop called Affordable Fashions, thinking it would augment my teaching income. I taught deaf and hard of hearing students and *loved* it. Even though I was well compensated, my teacher's salary was not enough to overcome our financial dilemma. Admittedly, I was very naive about this business venture. I didn't know that it takes an average of three to five years to establish a stable and profitable business. But "fools rush in", as the saying goes, and with no experience in retail sales, I dove headfirst with as much fearlessness as that Skycoaster ride.

Almost immediately, I noticed that the women who came to my shop were in my situation or worse. Often, customers would share their struggles, and I would interrupt to say, "Oh, I forgot to tell you, you're my fifth customer today so you get a free bag of clothes!" A total fabrication, but I felt empathy and if I could make someone's day a little better, I reasoned, that would be a good thing.

I continued to literally "give away the store" (not a sound business strategy) and I loved positively touching the lives

of women who were experiencing the same pains and challenges that I knew all too well. In those early days of starting this venture, I was driving in my car one day and having a conversation with God. Actually, the conversation was basically me bragging about a marketing tool I'd come up with that I considered to be quite brilliant and creative: a SMART Card for single moms entitling them to receive half-off all purchases on the last Thursday of each month.

"That's pretty clever, huh God?" I boasted. "SMART Card. That stands for 'Single Moms Are Real Treasures'." I named it that because that was the message I wanted to impress on each heart that entered my shop.

Well, if ever I've heard God's voice within my own heart, I heard Him say to me in that moment: *Sally, do you know that you're a real treasure?* A lump caught in my throat.

"No, I don't know that right now." My personal sense of femininity and worth had been shattered, but I sensed that if I continued to affirm other women's worth and beauty when they came into the shop, He would impart that to me, as well. With that divine nudge, my restoration had begun.

I carried on with my unsound business practices and - no surprise - continued to lose money. Almost one year to the day from my purchase of the shop, I went to a friend's son's graduation party. I sat across the table from an astute businessman and his wife, and shared with them about my resale store.

"You're not making money, you're losing money!" the gentleman said abruptly.

"I know but I love my shop," I rationalized.

"Why don't you become a nonprofit?" he suggested. "Obviously, you have a heart for helping women and if you become a nonprofit, you'll be more stable as an organization."

His suggestion seemed uncanny, as I'd been obsessing with this idea for a few months but didn't know how to make it happen.

"I'll walk you through it," he offered. Later that week, he gave me the paperwork and continued to meet with me weekly to help me complete it. He even introduced me to another nonprofit director. They treated me to lunch a few times, which was great in itself because I was so broke.

Within a few months, we had submitted and received nonprofit status. I renamed the store - drum roll, please - Treasure House Fashions. This name reflected all the *treasures* who shopped at the store every day. Suddenly, the heavens opened up and we had more donations than we knew what to do with. The overflow of merchandise filled my basement and I hosted sales out of my house almost every weekend. Our fledgling nonprofit needed more room and we began to seek additional space.

Our new location tripled our space and expenses. We literally took a leap of faith. That leap occurred more than 10 years ago and we've more than survived; we've thrived! In that decade, our facility expanded from 850 square feet to more than 6,000 square feet, only to outgrow that space, as well.

Today, Treasure House Fashions collaborates with more than 60 community organizations, and the number continues to grow as we link arms with additional service agencies. Almost 50 volunteers run the shop and we've established two part-time salaries. Most revenue is generated through sales, even

though 90 percent of our shoppers are SMART Card holders. The bargains are a blessing to any budget, and the sales enable us to distribute gift certificates to women through our agency partners. The shop is solid and our mission continues to expand.

"Do you know that you're a real treasure?"

Working with the women we serve has truly enlarged my heart. Despite my years of financial struggle, I can honestly say that I feel like one of the richest women on earth. My life has been enriched tremendously by sharing the challenging journeys of so many precious women.

When I got divorced, I thought it was the worst thing that could possibly happen. In reality, it was the springboard to abundant blessings for myself, as well as thousands of women. As the story turns out, my "picture perfect" plan was not even close to God's big picture of working "all things together for good."

Throughout my business, I've functioned far more from heart than head. I've also learned from experience that the heart can lead to wonderful places and teach valuable lessons. Here is what I've gleaned:

- The princess comes first (really!). Take care of yourself. It's not selfish, it's wisdom.

- Be as kind to yourself as you are to others.

- Multi-tasking is a fairy tale! Take one thing at a time and focus.

- Do the best you can with what you know. Paraphrasing Maya Angelou, "When you know better, you'll do better."

- Travel is wonderful but guilt trips should never be on your itinerary.

- Schedule your time to reflect your priorities. Work may be your passion but it's not your life. Relationships are your life!

At Treasure House Fashions, I often say that we feel like fairy godmothers. We wave a magic wand, change the outward appearance and release the treasure within. Running a nonprofit is hard work but what a joy it is! I had no idea that my dire personal situation could be transformed into a charitable mission that serves so many other women who have suffered similar misfortune.

It has transformed my own life in many ways, as well. I'm a healthier, happier person than when I started this great adventure. Cinderella not only survives but thrives... without the proverbial prince. I even get to go to the ball on my own terms and stay past midnight without my chariot turning into a pumpkin. Now that's a happily ever after that I can live with.

Clothing is the means – not the mission! Our
heart is to affirm the worth of each woman!

Sally Power is the founder and executive director of Treasure
House Fashions. Since 2000, this nonprofit resale shop has
served more than 10,000 women. Sally enjoys partnering
with businesses and agencies to affirm women, particularly
those in transition or crisis. She has received numerous
awards for her efforts and her story was featured in Woman's
Day Magazine. More than any award or achievement, Sally
is most proud of her three children: Nathan, Stephanie and
Chad. Watching them passionately pursue their dreams
despite challenges is the best legacy. Learn more at
thfashions.org.

Kim Lengling

"Don't tell God how big your mountains are; tell the
mountains how big your God is."

\- Joel Osteen

Chapter Six
AN UNEXPECTED JOURNEY

grew up in a small town in a single-parent home with one brother and two sisters. There was not a lot to do in our community so we made our own fun: flashlight tag, riding bikes, playing neighborhood flag football and building forts in the woods. My sisters and I quickly learned how to stick up for ourselves, especially if we wanted to play the same games as the boys.

Looking back on those years, I see my younger self as a stubborn yet determined tomboy who knew she could do anything and was willing to prove it. I was an average student and good athlete. I enjoyed spending time sitting alone in the quiet upstairs hallway of our home.

One month after graduating from high school, I entered the military. I was ready to leave my small town behind and looked forward to an adventure. As I boarded the bus and watched as my family and hometown disappeared behind me, I envisioned the exciting future that I was about to experience.

I arrived at Basic Training ready to take on the world. Men

and women were quickly separated, and I joined 38 other females who would be my family for the next several weeks. There was no privacy or quiet. We were together all day, every day - eating, sleeping, living and working. This was hard for me at first, as I was accustomed to having time to myself.

Most aspects of Basic Training came easy for me. I was in great shape and excelled with the physical conditioning. However, being a stubborn young tomboy, what came hard for me was the "keep your mouth shut, don't look your instructor in the eye, and obey all orders." As a new recruit, I learned to quickly adapt; I simply had to.

Graduating from Basic Training at age 18, I received a Top Secret security clearance and was assigned to Military Intelligence. I had a promising future filled with potential, so off to my first duty station I went. For the next three months, I was the only female at this location. Surprisingly, I missed my 38 bunk mates. The days on the base were routine: Wake up at 0500, shower, dress, go running, head to chow hall and then to my assignment. I spent most evenings in my barracks reading. I had a quiet building to myself and it became my refuge.

On a rare night out with a couple of friends, my world changed forever. I was verbally and physically threatened by two individuals. Forced to enter a vehicle, I was later sexually assaulted. Not wanting anyone to find out, I kept this traumatic event to myself. Who would I tell, anyway? Who would believe me? Keeping this secret began to wear on me mentally and psychologically. My daily routine became filled with fear and insecurity.

People around me noticed a drastic change in my demeanor and became concerned. I was encouraged to see the base chaplain. Eventually, I revealed the truth to him,

believing it would be kept confidential. It was not. Before I knew it, my commanding officer was informed.

Word spread around the base and all hell broke loose. I was subtly threatened by "friends" of my assailants, and two escorts were assigned to me for my own safety. My self-confidence and self-worth slowly diminished.

While things have changed significantly for females in the military, at that time it was not appropriate to take a stand or question those higher in rank. I was just an 18-year-old female trying to cope in a male-dominated environment. I knew that telling the truth and revealing the assault would be a huge personal risk for me. What I didn't realize at the time was the potential jeopardy to the long-term military careers of those who supported me.

I often wonder how I made it through that period in my life, young and on my own. Every day, I dealt with fear, depression, anger, anxiety and confusion. Instead of seeking support from my friends and family, I buried my emotions and locked the experience deep in my mind. I shared it with no one for more than 10 years, and continued to live my life as if that horrific experience of personal violence had never happened.

Eventually, I was honorably discharged from the military. I returned home and resumed life in my hometown. I reunited with my high school sweetheart, got married and soon had a beautiful daughter. Now an adult, my daughter and I share a very close and open relationship, and I have taught her to always be aware of her surroundings. Although I've never shared the details of the assault with her (until now), we have taken self-defense classes together and shared long talks about personal safety.

Years later, I found myself not sleeping well and having nightmares about those events from so long ago. I lost my appetite and began losing weight. I had built an invisible wall around me that no one could get through. I became bitter, unhappy, depressed and anxious. Trusting someone, anyone, was impossible. Nothing seemed to matter but the darkness that had settled upon me, concealing the scars that I would not let anyone see.

I discovered that the mind is an amazing thing. It has the capacity to take a painful event and lock it away in a secret compartment, but only for so long. When you least expect it, the door to that secret compartment crashes open. Make no mistake. It *will* crash open because it has to. Of course, I didn't know this at the time. Major events in your present life can trigger trauma from your past, causing nightmares, feelings of inadequacy, depression, fear, anxiety and lack of trust. Any of those things can be overwhelming. In my case, they can be and they have been.

It wasn't until years later while seeking counseling at the Veterans Administration that I learned I was experiencing Post Traumatic Stress Disorder, or PTSD. Darkness. That's what PTSD essentially is; darkness that sits in wait for the right moment to slam you. Going through an otherwise normal day, which always includes some level of stress, a dark memory can hit you from out of nowhere, throwing you off. By recognizing the memory for what it is, you can defeat it.

How very blessed I've been to have a wonderful veteran family that recognized the signs of PTSD within me, though they did not know the reason. They strongly encouraged me to seek help at the VA. I did so reluctantly because at the time, there were no female counselors available and to my knowledge, no one had dealt with my type of situation. I had to tell and retell my story, reliving the experience over and

over again. My journey at times has been very hard and emotionally draining.

Today, I consider that VA counselor my champion and friend, and continue to turn to him when the darkness creeps in. I know now that how I manage those feelings and who I turn to for support are crucial elements to my good mental health. The best way that I've found to keep those negative feelings at bay is to continue to grow in my faith, seek out my support system, stay busy and, most importantly, help others.

During this journey, my passion has become helping and supporting active duty military and veterans. As a part of my healing, I volunteer with a service organization that sends packages each month to our active duty military around the world. These care packets are filled with candy, snacks, letters and cards - a small taste of home and things that most of us take for granted. During the past 14 years, we have shipped more than 37,000 boxes. Yet the project is much more than sending boxes. I've had the opportunity to meet some amazing people and speak regularly to many wonderful organizations and groups.

Helping veterans and their families is what keeps me motivated. Having the opportunity to speak about PTSD and the struggles that may come with it for veterans and their families is a role that I did not envision for myself all those years ago when I entered the military. It is, however, one that I welcome. In my own small way, I can make a difference. With my support system and faith in God, I have that feeling once again that I had when I was very young: I can do anything.

PTSD does not go away but I have learned to manage it. One important thing that I've discovered is that demons will pop their dark heads out whenever I'm feeling hurt, angry,

anxious or fearful; what matters is how I face that trauma when it resurfaces. It would be very easy to let the darkness consume me. For some people, that may be what happens and for those people, I pray and encourage them to seek counseling. For myself, I am too stubborn to let the dark forces win. After all, I'm a very strong woman and I have a military background. Do I sometimes fall victim to feelings of inadequacy and depression? Sure I do, but I can now recognize them for what they are, face the battle and come out on the side with light.

"I consider that VCA counselor my champion and friend."

Sharing my story has not been easy. Writing it has brought forth memories and details that I'd rather erase forever. When I focus on the good that has come from this journey, I recognize how far I've come and how strong I can be. God willing, more good will continue to come with it. If revealing my struggles in written form helps even one female veteran - or anyone who has suffered from sexual or other kinds of abuse, for that matter - then sharing it will be more than worth it.

By embracing my circumstances and choosing to see the blessings, I have proven that the darkness does not have to win. Today, I am embarking on a new path and I know with my faith in God and my support system, it will be a good one. I've recently formed a non-profit organization called Embracing Our Veterans to provide low-cost and free services for veterans and their families who may not qualify for benefits through traditional means. Helping in this way sustains my healing process. I pray that the lessons I learned and the strength I've gained through my experiences can help ease the way for other veterans and individuals who suffer.

Isaiah 40:31
But those who hope in the Lord
will renew their strength.
They will soar on wings like eagles;
they will run and not grow weary,
they will walk and not be faint.

May God bless America, our veterans and each of you
reading this.

Kim Lengling *is a veteran whose passion is to help support veterans and their families. Her determination and drive have steered her toward achieving a new goal of co-founding a non-profit, Embracing Our Veterans, which provides referral services of area resources. Teaming up with local businesses and organizations, Embracing Our Veterans gives direction and guidance for veterans and their families for services from haircuts to health care. We can make a difference, one person at a time. To learn more, visit embracingourveterans.org.*

Laura Parker

"*The path to success is to take massive, determined action daily.*"

- Anthony Robbins

Chapter Seven
THRIVING, NOT JUST SURVIVING

*M*y perfectly beaded and tailored tulle wedding gown hung gracefully, waiting for me to slip into it and walk down the aisle towards the man I never thought I would find. It was the fall of 2007, and I was floating on a cloud of dream-come-true wedding day bliss. I didn't have pre-wedding jitters or a doubt in my mind. All I felt was excitement, happiness, peace and confidence.

As a 30-year-old successful woman, I didn't have the same insecurities that I would have had 10 years earlier. We had met in college, lived separate lives and found each other once again, at the right time. By now I knew what I wanted and had found all of it and more in Matthew, an amazing and wonderful man. I worked as a teacher after college, and lived on my own. I was always a planner and a saver and since I wasn't dating much in my twenties, I also worked part time as an artist and also as a personal assistant. Matt and I were both conscientious about saving money and not accumulating debt, but with my savings and part time income I was able afford a picture-perfect outdoor wedding at a country club without incurring any debt. On that day, surrounded by our dear friends and family, facing our bright

future, I felt incredibly blessed. It was like being in a fairytale with a handsome prince by my side. Nothing could dampen our spirits. It was everything I imagined it could be and the day breezed by too fast.

A fairytale wedding with my handsome prince.

After the reception we jetted off to an adventurous and memorable honeymoon in Maui, gifted to us from my boss as a going away present. I would not be returning to work there after the wedding because I was moving to Matt's hometown where he had a home and successful business. The week in Maui was amazing. We enjoyed our own little paradise and created memories that will last a lifetime. We spent hours just talking, daydreaming and planning out our lives as newlyweds. I felt so blessed and excited about the future. We were on top of the world together.

Our life of bliss crashed back to reality within days after returning home from our honeymoon when law enforcement came knocking on our door. We discovered that Matthew and his business had become the victim of identity theft. Some of the bizarre clues had been overlooked while planning the wedding, like traffic violations that arrived in the mail, and bills which didn't seem familiar. Suddenly we

became aware that these were not mistakes and discovered thousands of dollars fraudulently charged including houses, utilities, and numerous charge accounts that were growing. Assets were disappearing and debt was growing out of control. Our heads were spinning, trying to understand it all, and the financial ruin began to mount. It was overwhelming and devastating at the same time.

Matthew had spent years working to establish his good name, a home, a sound business and a secure life for us, and now it was gone. I became very sick and we learned that we were now expecting our first child. As the mounting financial hardships continued our security was now very unstable.

It was hard to believe that a few months earlier we were enjoying a lovely honeymoon after a dream-come-true wedding. Now I was sick, pregnant, jobless and selling some of our wedding gifts online in order to buy groceries. We both felt helpless.

It took a few months to sort out the identity theft. While some of the debt was "written off", we were financially responsible for a good part of it. The professionals advised us to file bankruptcy. We were told it was the only option and best way for us to ever really recover from such a selfish and destructive crime. This seemed so unfair. Even though the professionals shrugged at the idea of bankruptcy, it didn't seem like the right choice to us. We thought very hard about all we'd heard that morning and after a long discussion, prayer and some tears, we decided that we just couldn't do it. There was a nudge deep within our hearts from God that if we filed for bankruptcy, it wouldn't be good for us later on. So we went against what the lawyers advised us to do and did not file.

Jeremiah 29:11
"For I know the plans I have for you," declares the Lord, "plans
to prosper you and not to harm you, plans to give you hope
and a future."

With that decision and less than $500 to our name, it was
either give up or move on. We began our plan to start over.
We sold some appliances and scraped together $700, just
enough to rent a moving truck and fill the gas tank. We
packed our belongings and moved 400 miles back to where
I had previously been living and working. Seven month's
pregnant, I went back to teaching part time. Matthew started
a new business and worked every side job he could. We
felt good to be starting fresh, but we still struggled financially
trying to pay off the huge debts that had accumulated.

It was not the picture perfect life we had planned when on
our honeymoon. Our marriage struggled and our relationship
became as strained as our checkbook. Over the next several
years I often wondered if we would ever recover. Matthew
and I tried to keep the faith and believed that one day God
would make something beautiful from this mess.

Still, the day-to-day stress of financial hardship is a huge
obstacle to recover from. Our marriage over the next several
years became filled with anger, resentment, guilt, shame,
repeated setbacks, heartbreak, new insecurities and constant
frustration. But one hope remained: I knew that God loved
me and would never leave me. I held onto that through
every painful moment. I became increasingly depressed, as
did Matthew. Eventually, we sought professional help.

During this difficult time, we gave birth to another beautiful
daughter. Realizing that our precious girls depended on us
and deserved a happy and strong family, I decided that I
needed a new way of thinking and new approach to work.

Fueled with a new desire to repair our marriage and our finances, I launched my own business and began to work from home as a consultant and coach. Finally, out of the ashes came a beautiful creation that spurred me to dream bigger than I ever had.

It has been more than six years since we made that decision to avoid bankruptcy and start over. It has not been the dreamy journey I planned on my wedding day, and our finances are still not fully restored, but we've made a lot of positive progress. I read a magazine article recently which stated that financial ruin almost always ends a marriage, and most families don't survive that kind of stress, let alone thrive. Our goal is to thrive together and not just survive. We are both fully committed to each other and our daughters. We have forgiven the person who did this to us but we also have credit monitoring to ensure that it never happens again.

"God really did have his hand on us the entire time."

Today, Matt works as a public adjuster with building contractors and has his own roofing business. When he applied for his adjuster license we couldn't help but notice that one of the requirements was that he'd never filed for bankruptcy. What a miracle! At that moment, Matt and I looked into each other's eyes and knew that God really did have his hand on us the entire time.

Today my coaching and wellness business continues to grow and expand and I plan to open a wellness center for retreats and workshops. I've had the privilege of speaking at conferences for women who are discovering their purpose. Matt and I have been facilitating marriage workshops to

mentor couples who are struggling. I wonder if we'd be qualified for that calling had the early years of our married life been simple and worry free.

Matt and I still fondly remember our honeymoon on the blissful shores of Maui, when we were on top of the world. We plan to visit there again - only this time, we will have two beautiful girls with us and even more blessings to appreciate.

Laura Parker *is an author, coach, mentor and motivator. She is the founder of All Things Healthy Coaching. While overcoming life's obstacles, she discovered her passion to empower other women to achieve overall victory, success and balance in their own lives. She and her husband, Matt, have been blessed with two beautiful daughters. Laura is the author of two other books including All Things Healthy and Life, Love and Relationships: Reclaiming What is Yours and What God Intended. To learn more about Laura's workshops and access her healthy living recipes, visit allthingshealthycoaching.com.*

Susan Ceklosky

"Instead of looking at all the laundry you have to do, be grateful for the kids you need to do laundry for. Instead of getting frustrated waiting in line, be grateful for the extra minutes to not be racing. Instead of getting stressed at all the things you need to do, be grateful for all the things that need you. Instead of looking at what you haven't done, look at what you have. Life is perspective."

- Heather Frey

Chapter Eight
FROM GUILT TO GRATITUDE

From a very young age, I knew I would be a business owner. In high school I was president of the Future Business Leaders of America, and I studied nutrition and exercise science in college. When I was a senior, I found my dream job working as a fitness trainer for a new franchise called Curves for Women. It was the first Curves center in my state and I felt blessed to find a job doing what I loved at such a young age.

In fact, I loved it so much that I decided to open my own Curves franchise shortly after graduating from college. At age 23, with nothing but optimism, I hosted my grand opening. It took a while for the club to become known and profitable, so I waitressed at night to make ends meet.

Eventually, this new concept of women's circuit training caught on. Curves franchises were opening all over the country and soon I owned two thriving clubs. At age 28, I also had a great boyfriend, loving family and amazing friends. I traveled wherever I wanted and enjoyed life; but mostly, I worked from six in the morning until eight at night during the week, and a few hours on Saturday mornings. I was

passionately dedicated to my businesses and my days were filled with mentoring and motivating women to their goals.

Soon, I became engaged to my college sweetheart, Jim, who was secure and successful in his career as a chemical engineer. We got married and, soon after, were expecting a child and building our dream home. Our son Cole was born two days after we moved into our new home. Cole arrived two weeks early and was born with complications that were not life threatening but serious enough to keep him in the hospital for 10 days. The medical staff didn't want us to hold or touch him because of the IV's and oxygen; we were expected to visit him twice a day only.

So much to be grateful for.

I had made arrangements for maternity coverage at work, so I found myself with a hospitalized newborn and nothing but time on my hands while away from him. So after my morning visit with baby Cole, I went to work. My clients and staff thought I was crazy and should be home decorating the nursery or something, but I needed to keep busy and being around people was my way of coping with the situation. Jim

and I would go back to the hospital in the evening then I would drive to my other club to close up for the night. It was one evening while driving home that I felt my first stab of postpartum guilt.

Once we brought Cole home, things settled into a routine: sleepless nights, feedings every two hours, frequent diaper changes and many visits from family and friends. We felt extremely grateful to have Cole home after 10 days in the hospital. I must have kissed his forehead 1,000 times a day.

Cole slept most of the day, and although I loved holding him while he slept, sitting still gave my mind time to wander and think about work. It didn't help when I received a distressing call from a colleague saying that I was greatly needed at one of the fitness centers. Both clubs were growing fast and my staff was overwhelmed. I resented getting that call yet part of me was also a little excited. So I ended my maternity leave three weeks early and went back to working five hour days. I loved being back at work - the positive atmosphere, the upbeat music, and the interaction with clients who needed my support. My parents lived nearby and were thrilled to babysit their first grandchild while I worked.

Everything was not perfect, however; from day one I had intense feelings of guilt for leaving Cole. Even when I was happily coaching clients at the club and enjoying my time at work, it didn't feel quite right. I would think about Cole and wonder what kind of mother I was to go back to work so soon. I would tell myself that I chose to be a business owner and that my employees and clients depended on me. Arriving home every day, I would immediately feel guilty about not being at work. Transitioning my time between devoted mother and responsible business owner was difficult.

Over the next year, my postpartum guilt intensified. While at

work, I wished to be at home with my family. While at home, I thought about work. To make matters worse, the economy was declining and the fitness industry as a whole started to suffer. Profits were decreasing fast. Feeling frantic and wanting to avoid layoffs, I found myself putting in even more hours as I tried to generate new business.

Soon after Cole's first birthday, we discovered that we were expecting our second child. We were all thrilled and at the same time, a voice inside cautioned me: This work routine can't continue. I was being pulled in so many directions that I didn't know how I could possibly manage all of it with a second baby. Would my guilt be multiplied by two?

After a heart-to-heart talk with Jim and a serious review of our finances, we made some difficult decisions. With mixed emotions, we decided that I would sell one of the fitness centers and bring on a partner for the other to assume half the responsibility. This would decrease our income significantly, but hopefully the lessened demands on my time would allow me to spend more time being a mom.

These changes couldn't be implemented overnight; when baby Jake was born, I was still juggling everything. I arranged for time off and those weeks seemed to fly. This time when I returned to work, it felt like I had literally deserted my precious boys. When Jake was nine months old my mother called me at work with news that Jake had taken his first steps. I burst into tears, feeling like a horrible absentee mom. How could I have missed my baby's first steps? I was slowly falling apart from feelings of inadequacy and guilt.

Eventually we were able to downsize, which helped with work responsibilities but didn't alleviate my intense guilt. I then made another decision - not to change my schedule but to change my mindset. After some soul searching, I realized

that I was focusing on my frustrations and not my blessings. I was ignoring the power of gratitude. I had so much to be grateful for: two healthy children, a supportive husband, amazing parents, the best friends I could ever ask for, and work that I felt passionate about. My constant guilt was robbing me of the joy I should have been experiencing in my life. I made a conscious commitment to replace guilt with gratitude.

"Making the decision to stop being consumed by guilt changed my life."

I immersed myself in personal development books and motivational CDs which helped me focus on positive thinking. Like a light switch, something clicked and I began to see my life in a different way. I looked at my upcoming schedule and figured out what I could adjust and delegate. I blocked out time to put work aside and fully focus on being the best mom I could be. Making less money was acceptable because it meant I could fully enjoy my time with my boys. I continued to remind myself daily to be grateful. I was committed. I enjoyed my family when I was at home, and I enjoyed my work I was at the club. It changed my life!

I maintain a healthy balance to this day. I'm not perfect, but I do my best. My boys spend their days at school or with their grandparents while I'm at Curves or with clients of my new coaching business. I get to spend my days with women who want to be fit, healthy and fulfilled; most come to me feeling tired, depressed, unhappy, frustrated and guilty. Often they are stuck in a cycle of needing to take better care of themselves but feeling guilty for wanting to make their own needs a priority. I can empathize! I give them a big hug and

say, "It doesn't have to be this way. I promise that when you take good care of both your body and mind, you'll be an even better mom."

My friend and neighbor recently texted me a video of Jake, now six years old, riding his bike for the first time without training wheels. I could hear her cheering him on. He beamed with pride and excitement. I started to get a little choked up, wishing I could have been there. Then I flipped that feeling to one of gratitude. My son is happy, healthy and full of joy! I'm so blessed to have such an amazing friend who encourages him as if he is her own. I immediately felt an overwhelming sense of gratitude. When I arrived home that afternoon, Jake was so excited to show me what he'd accomplished. Instead of beating myself up, I celebrated with him.

Later that evening our family was gathered in the yard. I looked at Jim, our energetic little boys and our beautiful home. I thought of my parents, friends and clients. I reflected on everything I have to be grateful for, even my ability to enjoy life's many simple pleasures. Gratitude is a powerful tool and I vow to never waste another moment of my life feeling guilty. When I focus on the blessings, guilt is just not possible.

Susan Ceklosky *is a weight loss coach with Positively Fit U and a National Level Figure competitor. As a young entrepreneur, Susan opened one of the first Curves Fitness Centers in the US, a club that is still thriving today. Her bachelor's degree in nutrition is from Penn State University, where she minored in kinesiology. Her health coach certification comes from Cleveland Clinic. Susan is passionate about helping her clients boost their metabolism, lose weight and reclaim their energy. She lives in western Pennsylvania with her husband and two young sons. Download her free video at positivelyfitu.com.*

Donna Summers Moul

"Difficulties are what make life interesting; overcoming them is what makes life meaningful."

- Joshua J. Marine

Chapter Nine
STOP THE NEGATIVE MESSAGES

" $\mathcal{S}$ hare something about yourself that we wouldn't guess by looking at you." This request was part of an icebreaker exercise that I shared while facilitating a recent coaching group session with women. My thoughts returned to an earlier time in my life when I had begun my own healing journey.

I grew up in a quiet little neighborhood. I was the middle child, the "good little girl" in a family of six. My father was a building contractor and my mother, like most women then, was a full-time mom. I have many happy memories of spending quality time as a family, sharing meals, playing board games and taking our Sunday excursions to visit family and friends. In my town, I had more than a dozen cousins to play with after school and on weekends. We had the freedom to roam the neighborhood, explore in the woods and play our favorite games of dodge ball and cops and robbers. It was a carefree, happy time.

While there were advantages to growing up in the '40's and '50's, my childhood wasn't perfect. Children didn't have any rights back then. In my family, children were to be "seen and

not heard" (and sometimes, not even seen). It didn't matter what you wanted or needed, you did as you were told or there was a punishment. Along the way, I concluded that since what I wanted and needed wasn't important, I must not be important.

It was era of "father knows best." Daddy earned the money, made the important decisions and was the disciplinarian. "Wait until your father gets home!" was a menacing and effective threat. Fortunately, my father was kind and fair-minded. Usually, all he needed to do was give us a certain look or verbal remark and we paid attention; he rarely had to spank us. So I learned that men are important and powerful.

My mom was a good wife and mother, the epitome of selflessness. I watched her sacrifice her own wants and needs again and again in the interest of everyone else's. If there were four us and three pieces of pie, she was the first to give up her piece. "You go ahead," she'd say. "I'll do without." Everyone would agree that Mom was a wonderful and caring person; the underlying message that I learned from her, however, is that a woman's needs and desires don't matter.

Even though it was a much more innocent time back then, children in my day were bombarded with negative messages everywhere - at home, in school, at church and from society in general. Adults seemed to feel that it was their duty to continuously criticize children in an effort to correct their flaws and help them grow into moral, productive adults. "You're bad." "You're not deserving." "You can't do anything right." Children were told such things before they learned to have any defenses against them. We were taught to feel guilty for what we did and didn't do, and to feel shame for who we were.

At age 21, I married my childhood sweetheart. I was naive and ill prepared for this lifelong commitment yet expected to live happily ever after. I worked hard to be a good wife, mom, aunt and friend. To say that I was a people pleaser is an understatement. I was dancing as fast as I could to get people to like me. Throughout the years, I gave to my husband, my children, my friends, my community and more. I always put others first because no one ever taught me to give to myself.

As it turns out, this was not the life I had dreamed of as a child. I often felt overwhelmed and exhausted. I had no boundaries so I let everyone in, never saying no or expressing my anger. I wouldn't speak up when something bothered me and was always trying to fix things to keep everyone happy. Each time I swallowed my anger, I lost a little piece of myself. My frustration would build and build until I exploded over some minor incident; then, of course, I'd feel guilty and remorseful afterwards. If someone else was upset or unhappy, I believed that it was my fault. Over time, I became increasingly angry, resentful, depleted and depressed.

Finally one day, I realized that I was in trouble when I asked my husband to cut the grass and he replied that he didn't want to because he didn't want to clean up the dog dirt first. I didn't feel like I had a choice, so I reluctantly cleaned up the yard. Dog dirt was an accurate metaphor for how I felt about myself. I was in my early 30's and my life was out of control, I felt bad about myself, I had no power, and my marriage was on the rocks.

Around this time, my guardian angel, Luka, appeared in the form of a marriage counselor. After talking with my husband and me, she suggested that I join a women's support group to work through my issues. I was shocked to learn that I had *issues*; after all, I had tried so hard to do everything right. I

took Luka's suggestion and joined a local group. This is where I learned that I was co-dependent and that I was taking care of everyone else but no one was taking care of me. Although I was a grown woman, I was functioning like a child by repeatedly giving up my power in deference to my husband and family. History was repeating itself; I had become like Mom, a sacrificing wife and mother, putting everyone else's needs before my own.

> *"I married my childhood sweetheart and expected to live happily ever after."*

With the support of the group, I learned about the need for boundaries and how to protect myself. I learned how to say no (nicely) and speak up for myself. I learned how to express my feelings as an adult instead of swallowing my anger and acting like a child.

Most importantly, I discovered life-changing techniques that freed me from the negative messages I had absorbed as a child. I had been dragging them along with me, which damaged my self-esteem because I believed them to be true. These insidious and destructive messages become recorded in the brain and get replayed again and again, even when the people who instilled them in us are no longer around. Habits of self-criticism follow many of us through life and can be passed down to future generations unless we become aware of them and stop them. I have spent decades shedding such destructive messages, and it has improved my work as a therapist and now as a coach. Today, I work with women who are haunted by these messages from 30, 40 and even 50 years ago. My passion is to help women uncover and stop their negative messages

and reverse the unintended damage.

Learning how to set boundaries, change from co-dependent to independent, and eliminate old and irrelevant messages were the powerful gifts that I received through my support group. With healthy new habits in their place, I had the courage for the first time in my life to dream about the future. I faced my fear about going back to school. It was the early '70's and non-traditional students were flocking back to school. College opened up a whole new world to me. I discovered that I am smart (an amazing revelation at the time). My classes were informative, interesting and exciting. Psychology became my passion and later my career.

Since my three children were young at the time, I took one or two classes each semester. Ten long years later, I graduated and the local newspaper published an article: "Local Mom Graduates College 25 Years After High School." I was the first person in my family to graduate from college. My mom was so proud of me that she carried that newspaper clipping in her wallet for years.

Looking back on my life, I feel truly blessed. Even though I've had my struggles with low self-esteem and feelings of helplessness, I've learned so much from my group, my education, my life experiences and from my clients.

I've had three interesting and fulfilling careers. I think of my first one as having the luxury of being a full-time mom and homemaker for 25 years. For two people who didn't have a clue about how to parent, we've gotten great results! Our three wonderful children are intelligent, productive and compassionate. I love and respect them for who they are, for what they do and for how they live their lives. I couldn't be more proud, and I'm pleased to report that my husband and I are still happily married after all these years.

My second career was working at a mental health center. It was my training ground for becoming an empathetic therapist. I learned that I actually had valuable skills that I could use to help clients overcome their problems. I perfected the techniques of individual therapy and learned how to facilitate effective therapy groups. During this time, I also completed a master's degree in education.

After five years at the mental health center, it was time to venture out on my own and start my own counseling practice. My focus was helping women live their best lives. This is where the rewards for working through my co-dependency were realized through helping others who struggled with low self-esteem and feeling powerless. I provided hope to women by giving them tools to empower themselves. Since I drew from my life experience and not merely textbooks, I had instant credibility. Women whom I have counseled have gone back to school, left bad relationships, changed careers and claimed their right to live rewarding, fulfilling lives. Through individual and group therapy, I have taught hundreds of women to love and value themselves, own their strengths, set healthy boundaries, be assertive, say no and speak up for what they want and need. These were the important lessons I had learned in my own life. Most importantly, I have taught women that they don't need to be shackled by outworn negative messages they received while growing up. Awareness is the first step to change; then making the choice to give themselves more positive messages can occur and they can stop short of passing these destructive behaviors on to their children.

Recently, I launched my third career at age 69 as a certified life coach. I'm so grateful that, everything I've learned throughout my life has finally gelled; I get to inspire women to follow their dreams. My underlying belief is that the most important relationship you will ever have, other than the one

you have with your Creator, is the relationship you have with yourself. All other relationships will reflect how you feel about yourself.

Writer and publisher Louise Hay, whom I greatly admire, teaches us this: love yourself and you can heal your life. I know very well how important it is to be kind and loving to yourself, to be your own best friend. When women learn to do this, everyone benefits - including families, coworkers and entire communities. We all have the power within to stop the negative messages now.

Donna Summers Moul, MSEd, PC *is a certified life coach who is passionate about empowering women to discover their best lives. She spent 25 years working as a therapist in private practice. Through individual therapy, groups, workshops and numerous articles, she has helped hundreds of women learn how to love and value themselves. Donna offers individual coaching, coaching support groups for women, workshops and retreats. To learn more, visit Especially-For-Women.com.*

Julie Hundley

"The intuitive mind is a sacred gift and the rational mind is a faithful servant. We have created a society that honors the servant and has forgotten the gift."

- Albert Einstein

Chapter Ten
THREE KEYS TO CREATING A MAGICAL LIFE

I have always been interested in creating a magical life. With an understanding that we are the ones who often stand in our own way of success, I have taken this to heart. For the past 15 years, I have passionately worked on myself by honing my intuition, participating in transformational seminars, experiencing energy work, and learning from self-improvement tools, books and techniques. I'd like to share with you what I've learned along the way in creating a life full of miracles so that you, too, can create what you desire.

Miracles are waiting for you! Clarity is the first key. Every day, you have a choice in how you respond to situations and how you see your life. I invite you to take out a piece of paper and just think for a few minutes about the kind of life you want. Sometimes, we are clear on what we want; other times, our dreams can seem far off in the distance, barely visible.

In order to create a magical life, we must be able to envision our future story and be clear on the details. Do you realize that sometimes as the days go on, we continue to read from the same page in our book of life, and keep living the same way, while expecting different results? To turn our dreams into

reality, we need to know where we want to go.

How can you get clear on what you want? On your paper, jot down the first three things that pop into your head in response to this statement: I want [fill in the blank] in my life. These dreams could be as simple as finding a new friend or as big as taking an exotic vacation. By identifying what you're looking for, you're going to find it much quicker and easier.

Let me share a personal example. My second year of college, I was hired for a wonderful AmeriCorps Fellow position. AmeriCorps is like the domestic Peace Corps, and I would be working to serve the community through various projects. When a friend told me about the job, something inside of me said, "Yes! Do it! That's right up your alley!"

The interview went great and I was so excited to start. I'd have a 20-minute commute each day, so I needed to find a car quickly. At this juncture, most people would start entertaining thoughts like this: "It's too bad. That would have been a great opportunity, but there is no way I could buy a car on my non-existent salary, let alone being a student, and it could interfere with my class schedule. I'll just look for an on-campus job." Isn't it interesting that we talk ourselves out of success?

In order to have a magical life, it's important to be flexible and accept that change can be a good thing. It's necessary to not be so "set" and rigid with ourselves, our plans and our outlook on situations. Have you ever known someone who has a problem that they seem to focus on? They tell everyone about it, and that page in their book of life gets read over and over. It can even come up in casual conversations with people who are new acquaintances. The most interesting thing is what transpires when someone offers them a possible solution. All of a sudden, they claim

their problem. They own it with all of their heart and soul and identity. They do not want to give it up. They want to keep it! Others can support us in getting what we need or want, so it's important to be open to outside advice and guidance.

So, clarity is the first key. The second is remaining open to all possibilities, and accepting that your dreams are important enough to actually come to fruition. This acceptance comes from self-esteem. Have you ever felt like everyone else gets the lucky break or have you said, "Oh, that could never happen to me"? Watch your words. Manifesting miracles requires extending beyond mediocrity. Be brave enough to claim the new story that you desire and watch it become real.

The next day after my job interview with AmeriCorps, as I ate breakfast in my apartment, I said to my roommates, "I'm so happy to start my new job! All I need is a $1,500 dependable car." For me, clarity comes as I verbalize my thoughts, so I was thankful when those words tumbled out of my mouth. I had never purchased a car and hoped $1,500 wasn't a long shot.

That afternoon, as I was studying at the library for my final exams, all nestled between books and notes, I heard an almost audible prompting: Walk home now. Hmm, I thought, I have everything I need right here. You see, at that moment, many people (if they recognized that they'd heard a prompting) would think, Isn't that odd. Now why would I ever return home when I have this important final and I have everything I need right here? In my case, that thought only lasted a split second because I depend on the Divine. I've learned to *trust* instead of question, and to *act* instead of second guess. I stood up and gathered my things.

As I made my way back to the apartment, the sky was bright

blue. The flowers were coming up and the sun was shining. I was so happy. I loved my life! Lost in thought, I walked right past a blue Honda with a sign in the window: For Sale - $1,500.

I was about 10 steps past the car when it registered in my mind that this was the miracle I'd asked for just six hours earlier. I couldn't believe it but, at the same time, I could.

"I invite you to dream big, take action and expect results. The sky is the limit."

Many times, we believe that we need to do it alone, that being responsible and dependable means having a plan and sticking to it - regardless of what you feel, or even being open to the possibility that things could change. When we believe that independence reigns, we are often left alone and hopeless. Life can seem overwhelming and the hours in the day impossible to match our mounting task list.

So, the third key is depending on the Divine. Creating a magical life is not up to us alone. It's actually impossible, in my opinion. I believe that I co-create my life with God. You see, I believe we are here to learn this co-creative process and witness the daily miracles that arise from being in tune with a higher power. Each of us holds the answers to one another's dreams, hopes and challenges. I've found that when I'm open and depending on those divine messages and promptings, my life is an amazing ride. It's rich with scenery, relationships, experiences and miracles, and it usually unfolds much better than I could have ever imagined for myself. People cross my path who give me the answers I'm looking for, and I use my intuition to tune into my higher

guidance. This is all part of what creates the "magic."

There are many ways to manifest miracles in your life. Here I have addressed three that I have used throughout my life to co-create all sorts of amazing things. More recently, in the last few years, I've gone from financially broke to creating a six-figure business, to leaving a challenging neighborhood by finding the perfect renter for our home, and then to manifesting a dream home. I invite you to dream big, take action and expect results. The sky is the limit! Be a player in the game of life and not a referee on the sidelines. When you apply the three keys to creating miracles in your life, I can promise that your life will change in the most wonderful ways. Miracles are waiting for you! I guarantee it.

Julie Hundley *empowers women to listen to their intuition so they can thrive in all areas of their lives. A graduate of the Institute for Integrative Nutrition, Julie is a certified health coach trained in many healing modalities. Julie is in the top tier of leadership in dōTERRA Essential Oils and leads a large team of dynamic leaders & wellness advocates. Passionate about empowering others to experience wellness, she spends her time sharing health and wellness resources with families around the country. She is the author of the upcoming book "10 Keys to Manifesting Miracles & Creating a Life you Love." Julie and her husband, Nick, reside in Utah with their four children. Learn more at JulieHundley.com.*

Jennifer Drake Simmons

"If you can dig deep and find strength, you can win."
— Jennifer Drake Simmons

Chapter Eleven

WHERE THERE'S A WILL THERE'S A WAY

*W*hen faced with adversity, there are only two things you can do: surrender or fight. If you dig deep enough and find your inner strength, you can overcome any situation.

I met my husband, Brian, when I was just 15. We dated for 10 years and things were playing out perfectly. He had an exciting career playing Major League baseball, I was a successful event planner and we were planning our dream wedding. Life was good and I felt blessed.

Soon after we married, Brian began to struggle with various injuries and was being bounced around to different teams all over the country while I was at home alone. The hope of him continuing in the Major Leagues seemed to be dwindling so we needed a new plan. When we discovered that we were expecting our first child, Brian turned in his bat for a baby! Finally, we were both living in the same city. Brian returned to college and before we knew it, he graduated and landed at a great job.

I had a rough delivery but we were blessed with a healthy

baby boy, Will Harrison. Once again, things seemed perfect until Will was two years old. One spring morning, the day began as usual at our family's cabin in the woods. We were headed out for our usual walk to the pond to see the fish, one of Will's favorite things to do. As soon as Will reached the edge of the water, he fell to the ground. At first it looked like he had fainted. Brian picked him up and I got a glimpse of his face. His eyes had rolled back and he'd begun to drool. He was unresponsive in Brian's arms. We were terrified - in the middle of the woods with no phone reception to call 911 and no clue what was happening to our son.

In a panic, I ran to the cabin and kept dialing for help until I finally got through. I was overwhelmed with fear of losing my sweet Will. At the same time, I was three months pregnant and terrified about the stress I was putting on my unborn baby. The 911 dispatcher was concerned that the cabin was in a remote area with no official address. While I explained how to find us, I could see Brian trying to wake up Will. Finally, he let out an innocent cry and opened his eyes. A surge of relief flowed through me. Will was responsive but his skin felt hot, as if he had a high fever. We breathed a deep sigh of gratitude when the ambulance finally arrived. After what seemed like hours, we reached a small community hospital.

The emergency room doctor discovered that Will had a slight ear infection and a temperature of 102. "A sudden fever in a young child can sometimes cause a febrile seizure," he explained. Will was given fluids and we were sent home in a few hours with instructions to see a neurologist.

The neurologist confirmed that febrile seizures are a common occurrence in young children. His concern was that the incident usually causes the body to go stiff and Will did not do that; he went completely limp. Just to be safe, the doctor prescribed an anti-seizure medicine for us to have on hand

24/7 in case Will experienced another seizure.

Will returned to being a healthy, active, growing boy. We continued on with our lives and our second son, Blake, joined our family. Two years later, Brian and the boys were playing in the family room while I cooked dinner. Will suddenly jerked up from his knees and fell to the floor convulsing.

"Will's having a seizure!" Brian shouted.

I rushed over with the medicine, but before it was necessary to administer, Will stopped seizing. We looked at each other, stunned and feeling devastated by what had just happened. Over the next few months, we faced multiple doctor appointments and Will endured numerous medical tests, as he'd begun to experience seizures daily. What was happening to our little boy?

One of the tests that the doctors ordered was a diagnostic 24-hour video EEG. Will and I packed up for a sleepover at the hospital and Brian stayed home with Blake. Twenty electrodes were glued to his head so the monitor could capture any seizure activity. The technicians recorded six seizures in the first few hours. After those test results came back, Will was officially diagnosed with epilepsy. We were shocked but grateful to have a formal diagnosis. A team of neurologists stepped into action and mapped out a treatment plan. Will would have to take anti-seizure medication every day to control his seizures. We put our trust in this treatment plan and were hopeful that it would work.

Our optimism was quickly dashed as soon as Will began this course of treatment. His condition worsened but the medical team assured us that by slowly increasing the dosage, he would overcome it. We continued for several weeks stacking up to the optimal dose, only to realize that the medication

was causing more seizures and, on top of that, horrible side effects. We spent weeks weaning him from this drug before trying another. In the meantime, our poor Will was averaging 30 seizures a day and was regressing at an alarming rate. In a daze most of the time, he was no longer able to attend preschool or participate in any sports or strenuous activities.

"I was not going to stop until Will's seizures numbered zero."

Brian and I felt like we were living in a nightmare and our child was a laboratory rat. We were gravely concerned that these drugs could cause a host of serious lifelong issues. After a while, Brian and I decided we needed to find the right treatment for our precious son. We were not even close to surrendering. The fight was on. We spent every free moment doing research about epilepsy. We sought information from hospitals, libraries, medical journals, websites and case studies. Some days, it felt like I was in medical school. Will needed a cure and we were determined to find it.

Our nightmare continued without abatement. Will was seizing so often that he couldn't be left alone. Thankfully, our parents, siblings, neighbors and friends all helped out. He was four-and-a-half years old at the time and he seemed like a newborn. His seizures would cause him to drop his head uncontrollably, sometimes hitting it on whatever hard surface was in proximity. Since Will could not sit at a table, we had picnics on the floor for every meal. Play dates, swimming, trips to the park, walking down stairs were all too dangerous. I was nervous about everything and we began to focus on things that were safe for him. I used food as a distraction to make him happy. It was safe and he was "allowed" to eat.

Ten grueling months later after hundreds of seizures and five failed medications, Will was admitted to Children's Hospital. For the next five days, neurologists closely monitored his brain while experimenting with a variety of intravenous medications. Every single one failed. Brain surgery was not an option. Perplexed, the doctors admitted that there was nothing left to try and we were released from the hospital. Brian and I were exhausted, overwhelmed and felt hopeless.

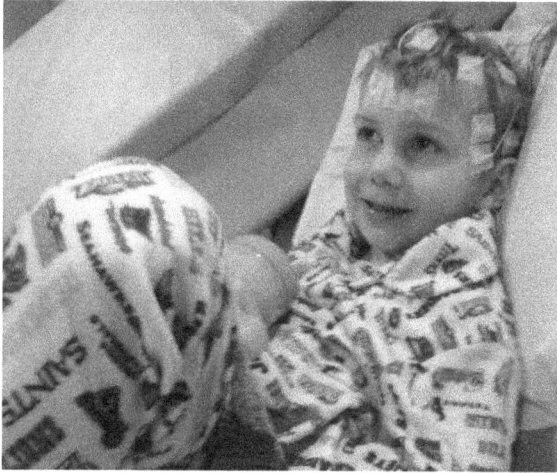

Will during a 24 hour EEG.

During that hospital stay I came across an article about a nutritional treatment that had been used in children with uncontrollable epilepsy. We spoke to Will's neurologist about it and she agreed it was worth a try. After all, it seemed to be our only hope. While tapering off the medications, we started to make some changes to Will's diet. After limiting carbohydrates and increasing fats and proteins, we noticed an immediate improvement. Before long, he was down to 15 seizures a day. We were thrilled but I was not going to stop until that number dropped to zero.

Through our research, I also learned about the ketogenic diet, an extremely strict regimen that has to be initiated in a

hospital setting. We procrastinated on trying this diet because it meant that Will would have to fast for three or four days. He had already been through the ringer and we didn't want another hospital stay or to deprive him of food - one of the only safe things he could enjoy. However, I knew in my heart that Will needed this diet. Overall, we loved the medical staff and had confidence in the dietician who we had been with over the years. For reassurance that we were doing the right thing, we decided to get a second opinion from a specialist at another hospital. I took a chance and emailed a summary of Will's medical history to this doctor. I was pleasantly surprised when I received a reply from him at ten o'clock one Friday night. His professional opinion was that Will start the ketogenic diet right away. Our decision was made, but now we had to "starve" our dear son. We knew what we had to do, but we were very reluctant to withhold food from our child.

Then suddenly, Will spiked a high fever and we rushed him to the ER (they are dangerous for children with epilepsy). He was critically ill and I was more scared than I'd ever been. After four days in the hospital, we learned that he had salmonella poisoning. Bewildered, we tried to figure out how this had happened. We realized that amongst the high fever, vomiting and diarrhea, we had not witnessed any seizures. Will had not eaten for more than four days and his seizures had stopped. Yes, he was pale and very weak but not seizing. The illness put his body in starvation mode, which is precisely what the medical journals indicated that we needed to do to begin the ketogenic diet. I silently joked that I never thought I'd be so happy to see my son get food poisoning!

After Will's neurologist made her rounds later that day and gave us the thumbs up, Will was able to begin this regime. This was our turning point after two long years; the seizures

had ceased. As it turns out, Will had not been starved to death but starved to life. We had our son back!

Even though the diet was extremely strict, it was our miracle. Every morsel of food needed to be weighed, measured and eaten in its entirety in order for the diet to be successful. Will has been a trooper. On top of being deprived of certain foods, he's had to ingest numerous supplements and concoctions that would quickly turn anyone's stomach. We also tested his urine daily and his blood monthly to ensure key nutritional levels were met.

Every year since Will was diagnosed, we walk in the Epilepsy Foundation's Fun Run/Walk with our amazing and supportive friends and family. We asked Will to name our team and help design our T-shirts. He chose Will's Warriors and wanted a shield to symbolize his fight against the bad guys in his brain. Together, we decided on the motto, "Where there's a Will there's a way!"

We were lucky enough to find the strength needed for our family's battle against epilepsy and although things are not perfect, they are pretty close. We hope that our healing journey as a family inspires others to not give up until a solution is found. We followed our hearts, and with Will, we found a way.

Jennifer Drake Simmons is a devoted mom and author of an upcoming book about her family's battle to save their son from epilepsy. She is a graduate of Virginia Tech, active in her community and raises funds for the Epilepsy Foundation. She and her husband live in western Pennsylvania with their two young sons. She offers support, encouragement and resources for families living with epilepsy at WillsWay.net.

Marylu Zuk

"The learning curve never ends for any of us."

\- Marylu Zuk

Chapter Twelve
HOW CAN I PUT THIS NICELY?

I used to keep a quote by Ralph Waldo Emerson posted on my desk at work: "Your actions speak so loudly, I cannot hear what you say." It was a reminder that people - in this case, one of my staff members - sometimes nod their way through a discussion then turn around and repeat the same behavior they just talked about changing. Presenting helpful information to someone you manage or supervise is often met with resistance, or even ignored. I am known to be a comedienne with a dry sense of humor. I sometimes fantasize about creative ways, although inappropriate, to respond to issues at work. For example, how fun would it have been to send a letter like this:

Dear Miss Iwanna B. Taken-Seriously,

Following our repeated conversations regarding your desire to be seen as a professional by your coworkers, I have come to the conclusion that in reality you do not. The fact that I am once again addressing the topic of your cleavage in the workplace leads me to believe that our previous discussions were clearly not clear enough.

Perhaps you are more of a visual than auditory learner, and seeing it on paper will help solidify this feedback and allow you to read the words over, and over, and over, in hopes that they sink in. So here's a suggestion: Before you leave the house each morning, look in the mirror! I assume you have a mirror based on your skillfully painted visage and blown-out coif, but I digress.

Look in that mirror and follow these five simple steps:

1. Bend forward at the waist 45 degrees (that's a single slice of an eight-cut pizza, if math is not your forte).
2. Now, lift your head and look in the mirror.
3. Notice the area about three inches below your neck.
4. If you see clothing fully covering your breasts, grab your keys and get to work, girlfriend.
5. If you see cleavage, change your outfit and repeat the process.

While you mumble under your breath (I'm not stupid) and rant about my prudish and puritanical rules, keep in mind that there are plenty of places where cleavage is completely acceptable - indeed encouraged - in the workplace. This just isn't one of them.

If you would like a letter of recommendation to attach to your hoochie-coochie application, you may see Human Resources on your way out. Otherwise, I assure you this is the last time this discussion will transpire.

Sincerely,
R. Dey-Covered

Okay, first of all, the answer is "no." Of course, I have never sent such a letter but I assure you that I wanted to on many occasions. And lest you think I need to proclaim that names have been changed to protect the innocent, alas, many names would need to be changed, as this was not a one-person, one-time occurrence.

Having spent nearly three decades working for two companies (an anomaly today), I tired of spending the bulk of my time adjusting the behaviors of those choosing to revolt against basic expectations. If you're thinking that's a brusque approach, you just don't me well enough yet.

"If your breasts are fully covered, grab your keys and get to work, girlfriend."

In reality, as a leader, I am an inherent nurturer, an innate Pollyanna. I choose to look at every challenging situation from a positive perspective and focus on the best solution. Fundamentally, I want to help people become better - better employees, better salespeople, better workers. Any coach (sports or otherwise) will tell you that in order to help someone improve, you must first meet them where they are then clearly explain where they should be. If you are an effective leader, you will describe the steps they must take to get from where they are to where they should be. Of course, along the way you would be providing positive reinforcement and encouraging feedback.

As often as people deny having thin skin, when it comes to constructive communication and helpful advice, some people naturally revert to their inner child. While I agree it is no fun to be corrected, it is much simpler in the long run to be open-minded to suggestions for improvement than to

maintain some false sense of perceived perfection in the workplace. This concept is fully digestible when it comes to the other guy; however, when it comes to identifying, admitting and rectifying our own shortcomings, the sting of feedback can initially make some of us squirm and bring others to tears.

The last thing I want to do is reduce someone to tears. Anywhere. Ever. Especially at work. (Note to self: work on that.) While I've never had that reaction to constructive feedback at work (though I have with other stuff), I most certainly squirmed on many occasions.

One form of communication that I still struggle with to this day is leaving a succinct voicemail. (If you're reading this and you've ever worked with me, I know, you're nodding your head with those wide eyes that speak volumes. As in "'you have no idea!")

"Hi, this is Cara Concise. I need to speak with you. Please return my call. 555-123-4567."

Yeah, I'm sorry, that just isn't happening. I like details. I need to know specifics. I need you to know the specifics, too. My message would sound more like:

"Hi this is Willa B. Wordy. It's 10:22 on Tuesday, January 24. I was calling to speak with you about [insert specific topic]. Hopefully we can connect by (insert deadline) so I can (insert statement to affirm urgency of returning the call). My number is 555-123-7890. I'll be available most of the day except between 3:30 and five o'clock when I'll be in a meeting. But any time before 3:30 or after five would be great. Thanks! [Pause and think about what I might be forgetting.] Again, it's Willa B. at 555-123-7890."

Okay, don't hate me. Admitting that I have a problem is the first step, right? How did I know this was a problem? At first I would catch references to Marylu's marathon messages, or I would get frustrated return calls saying something like, "You left me a message but the machine cut you off," with a heavy emphasis on *the machine cut you off*. And eventually I would chase someone down for information I'd requested and the response would be loud and clear: 'I started listening to your voice mail but lost my train of thought."

"The learning curve never ends for any of us."

I'm embarrassed to say that I had to hear this multiple times before it finally sunk in. So I, like others, don't always adjust my behaviors the first time either.

Having managed, mentored and guided many, I have learned these truths:

- Not everyone looks at things from the same perspective.

- Past experience shapes current behaviors.

- The learning curve never ends for any of us.

We are all human, and humans err. By recognizing our errors and correcting them, we grow both as individuals and professionals in the workplace. I am not suggesting that you relish your errors or seek to increase them in number, but I can assure you (from experience) that when you attain a level of professional confidence in which you can say aloud, "It was me, I take responsibility, I was wrong," then a weight will lift. Humbly pronouncing that you are human and, as such, you

occasionally mess up is an indicator of professional maturity. Simply put, you see where you botched things and take appropriate measures to resolve/change/fix the issue.

Arghhh! Admitting those mistakes! It's like pulling a genuine "I'm sorry" out of a four-year-old. Go out on a limb and try it. You will find that you gain supporters, along with that ever elusive respect, when you are willing to admit responsibility for failed attempts. Being publicly accountable for results (or lack thereof) models to others that it is okay to try, to risk, to act. Outwardly recognizing that you are your perfectly imperfect self supports this.

If you always expect and only accept perfection, others will restrict their creativity and hold back. Balancing high expectations with a nurturing workplace environment takes a bit of finesse.

Now before I get back to finessing, let me find those other unsent letters I tucked away for another story, another day.

Marylu Zuk, *founder of M.L. Zuk Consulting, works with companies and organizations to champion teams toward reaching their goals. Using humor and a Pollyanna attitude, her top priority is keeping people energized in the workplace. She spent the early part of her career in the sometimes-friendly skies before life's path led her to other roles: road warrior, sales manager, trainer, consultant and higher education enrollment VP. Her first book, Whose A&& is That?, promotes women's positive self-image, storybook style. Learn more at maryluzuk.com.*

Mary Limbacher

"I've learned that people will forget what you said, people will forget what you did, but people will never forget how you made them feel."

- Maya Angelou

Chapter Thirteen

FILLING MY OWN SHOES OF DESTINY WITH COMPASSION

In the fall of 2007, a decision to help a friend led to a most life-altering outcome. I visited Zelienople, Pennsylvania, a small town near my home to help a friend and trusted confidant open a new business. Kristi has wonderful energy and her creativity knows no boundaries. I've never been known as a half-hearted friend or one to ignore an opportunity to solve a problem. Rescuer, peacemaker, and caretaker… these are roles in which I excel.

Even though I was excited about Kristi's venture, I allowed my mind to fantasize about my own business dream of opening an autism support center. For 16 years, I was a stay-at-home mom to my two sons. During that time I wrote a monthly column for a local community magazine and occasionally painted freelance murals. As my boys grew more independent, this lifestyle had reached its best-by date. During the 20-minute drive from my house to Kristi's shop, I envisioned my future nonprofit center, which would be the first of its kind in our area. I saw it as an extension of a support group I founded seven years earlier with the encouragement of another friend, Linda. She was the first parent I'd met who

had a son diagnosed with Asperger's syndrome, just as my older son, Andy, was in the middle of fifth grade. She inspired me to form the group so that we could meet other families.

Since Linda lived in Zelienople, she met me at Kristi's shop. As Kristi answered the door, my optimism shifted as I saw my friend's expression, blank with resignation. She could not open her business due to a number of overwhelming circumstances, which couldn't be fixed by one well-meaning friend. With that, Kristi asked if I was interested in sub leasing her space. Could I handle the rent? Would the tiny space, minus any real storage area serve my imagined needs? Would I mind sharing the bathroom with the barbershop that was connected?

Ah. There was the deal breaker. Not in a million years!

Linda pointed to a space for rent across Main Street. I headed over in anticipation only to peer into the darkened, narrow retail space. Then, without a hint of trepidation - which looking back, surprises me - I immediately saw an opportunity to provide to others the compassion that I wished my family could have experienced to individuals living with autism and their families. The furniture that was needed to bring this space to life began to align in my mind's eye, and the possibility of realizing my dream roared in my ears.

Feeling an overwhelming sense of hands on my back, gently pushing me to take the risk, I made the decision. I would not be deterred. Over the course of the next several weeks, I gathered a few trusted friends and convinced the landlord, an insurance company, and myself that despite having no real business expertise or any sufficient funding, this vision was going to happen.

When the lease was ready to sign, I finally told my husband,

John, fearing that he would talk me out of what I viewed as my calling. For as long as I could remember, I felt that I had lived to fulfill everyone else's needs before my own. Having children and going to zoos, museums, and play dates was the happiest time in my life. Now, I needed to make a unique contribution so that families would have a place to find help. Despite the risk, I'd dust off my bachelor's in journalism and open Parents in Toto Autism Resource Center in January 2008.

That summer while on vacation at Hershey Park, John bought last minute concert tickets. Sharing the rock bands Heart, Cheap Trick, and Journey with Andy and our younger son, Daniel, was a bonding between the generations that couldn't have been more rewarding. I don't remember ever being as big a fan of 80's rock music as I was that night.

After the concert, we made our way down the stadium benches. We neared the stairs leading to the safety of the grass field. Out of the corner of my eye, I saw my older son Andy attempt to jump the steel railing as a shortcut or maybe to inject some energy into his rested muscles. He would have cleared the four-foot rail if the tip of his running shoes hadn't caught the rounded top. He crashed onto the hardened ground five feet below and rolled over clutching his ribs, trying to catch his breath. At that moment all the blood seemed to rush to my heart that was about to burst with terror. As I bent down to bring him into my arms a security guard began to fire questions at Andy.

"Why did you jump the fence? Is your face always that pale? How old are you?" I panicked, thinking that the guard assumed Andy was under the influence. I flew into a protection mode that would have made any past defenseman on the football field in front of us proud.

Andy was still struggling to catch his breath when he

responded, "I don't go outside much."

I blurted out, "He has autism." The words seemed to surprise me as much as it did the guard. After an exchange of explanation, she seemed satisfied that the behavior was more related to the diagnosis and less about underage drinking.

Andy was immediately furious after hearing me use his diagnosis as a crutch. A feeling of inadequacy overwhelmed me. I tried to apologize and explain my knee-jerk reasoning to Andy for elevating his autism as an excuse, all the while knowing that we narrowly avoided a trip to the police station. He refused to allow me to justify my logic.

As I walked alone with my deflated thoughts surrounded by hundreds of families, unaware of what just happened, I flashed back to my days as a young girl defending my brother who has Down's syndrome. At an age much younger than Andy was on that night at the concert, I recalled staring down other mall-goers when they caught sight of Michael's face. His Down's features were fodder for unwanted stares and uneducated comments to which I would go into attack mode, just as I did at Hershey Park.

This need to advocate, defend and cultivate awareness and understanding of differences, to protect those who deserve to have happiness without judgment, had developed in me at an early age after my mother died. Her death at the age of 42 stirred another powerful desire of mine as a parent: I wanted to truly know my boys and for them to know me as their mom.

On Easter Sunday in 1968, I can vividly recall the tiny hospital room where my mother lay propped up in her hospital bed. From my four-foot vantage point, she seemed to be much

too high to reach. Her dark hair wildly surrounded her pale, gaunt, skeletal face. Her appearance horrified me. My older and younger brothers, Michael and John, and my younger sister, Margaret, my father, and several uncles acted as if young children visiting their mom in a cancer ward was an everyday occurrence. Everyone, including the nurses, tried to make the visit light-hearted, almost party-like.

At the age of seven, I was confused, frightened, and enraged. I finally addressed the elephant in the room, "Mommy, why do you look so funny?"

My uncles quickly steered the conversation to topics of my dress and how tall I had gotten. I now know this was all to distract my mom from the inevitable; she only had weeks to live. Physically ravished over the previous year by ovarian cancer, she maintained an amazing amount of courage. That one visit would be our last as my father made the decision to lovingly protect us from knowing anything more until after the funeral. Returning to school just weeks after learning of my mother's death, I wanted to be invisible to the unwanted stigma of being the only student in my class without a mom.

I've been trying to fill my mother's shoes since I was a young girl.

Starting off a new school year in second grade proved to be much worse. My teacher, a self-appointed town crier, announced loudly to another teacher that I was the little girl whose mother had died. She even pointed me out in the front of the line. Did she think I couldn't hear her? Heartbroken and missing my mom, I felt a horrifying embarrassment and a profound lack of compassion at that moment. After her callous comment, I looked at the wall by the door and thought; *I am no different than this light switch, an unfeeling, utilitarian object.*

I would experience many similar incidences over the coming years where I felt belittled, judged, and neglected. A money hungry caregiver who should have protected and even comforted my siblings and me treated me as insignificant. As I got older I came to realize that these deeply felt hurts taught me the importance of empathy, a profound life lesson. Even at a young age, I could see that treating children this way was wrong.

"Each heartache was matched by a gift from God."

Looking back, I believe that I was being strengthened and shaped to be able to handle my destiny. Each heartache was matched by a gift from God. The very week of the funeral, a couple moved into the house next door. Joyce recounts the first meeting when, followed by my sister, I stood at her fence and announced that our mom had just died. She opened her heart to years of afterschool conversations and the unconditional love that I so craved. Her ever-present interest, compassion and four decades of friendship have been one of the greatest gifts in my life.

Today, I am grateful for my awakening from an unfocused life to one where I matter. I am also grateful for the strides Andy and Daniel have made: driving, having friends, going to college. For too many years I felt imprisoned by those unbearable wounds of my childhood not knowing how to defend myself. If not for my past, I would not be the compassionate woman I am today.

Being active in a purposeful life uplifts me. My life experiences have allowed me to relate better to children and adults who visit Parents in Toto. I still vividly remember my experiences as a seven-year-old child who lost her mom, the sister of a young man with Down's syndrome, and a parent of a son with autism. My gift was overcoming the challenges that would forever adjust the course of all of our lives. Fortunately, the mutual inspiration and compassion I experience with other individuals across the generations and economic divides knows no boundaries. I am blessed because of my trials, not despite them.

Mary Limbacher inspires ideas, information, and hope for hundreds of individuals and families living with autism. The founder and director of Parents in Toto Autism Resource Center in Zelienople, Pennsylvania, her center hosts various support groups, creative activities and professional speaker events. Mary motivates her visitors to develop friendships; learn skills toward rewarding vocations; and, embody confidence and generosity of spirit. She has been recognized for her humanitarian efforts by receiving a Jefferson Award and ACHIEVA's Excellence in Community Awareness Award. Mary dreams of a society that appreciates individuals' differences and celebrates their contributions. Share in Mary's vision at parentsintoto.org

Helen Baratta

"*Everyone thinks of changing humanity and nobody thinks of changing themselves.*"

\- Leo Tolstoy

Chapter Fourteen
EMBRACE CHANGE, SAY YES

Rules work for me. I follow recipes to the letter, enjoy sewing with patterns and detailed instructions, and even changing the oil in my car every 3,000 miles. Working in the corporate world, it became apparent to me early on that making too many exceptions to the "rules" leads to trouble down the road. Ironically, I struggle with following the rules in one important area of my life: my health.

As a teenager, I began an unhealthy journey that took decades to reverse. I started smoking cigarettes at age 14 when my parents divorced. Living with my dad and stepmother opened up a world of new experiences and challenges. I lived in a house where drinking and smoking marijuana was acceptable, not only for my parents and their friends, but also for me, my siblings, and our friends. In my dad's crazy way of thinking, we were responsible with our alcohol and drug use as long as we could fulfill our responsibilities outside the house. At age 16, I was a National Honor Society student, worked a fast food job after school and spent most of my free time numb to the world as a closet drug user.

I had a harder time functioning at the higher level that was expected during my college years. I struggled to maintain a healthy balance of working my way through college and maintaining an enviable party life. Once I met my sweet husband, Vince, finishing my studies so that I could be with him became more important than partying. Vince was not a fan of cigarettes, so after 10 years of smoking, I had my last cigarette on our wedding day.

I cleaned up my act and began a blessed life with a wonderful husband and our two sons. I had a successful career working in health insurance. Unfortunately, something else had become my drug of choice: food. My weight steadily increased as I coped with life by using food. The scale tipped 200 pounds during my second pregnancy and that was only the beginning.

I am thankful to have a husband who loves me just as I am. Fat or thin, Vince loves me. His career as a contract engineer moved us all over the country. With each move, I would lose weight beforehand then gain it back after we were settled in a new location. Something was missing and I was filling it with food.

When we moved once again to a new hometown in 1998, a new friend, Jane, invited me to church. I was resistant. God was one of the things I left behind when my parents divorced. I spent years trying to numb the memories of Sunday school and Bible camp. Was I still mad at God about my parent's divorce? Could there be something at church that I was missing? Jane didn't give up. After two years, I finally agreed to go to church with her, and it was eye opening. I rediscovered the love that I felt as a little girl in a Baptist church, where I first met and accepted Jesus. I had found what I was missing: a relationship with Christ. Jesus loves everyone, I rediscovered: even big, fat me.

I had a lot of making up to do in my spiritual life, so I became a super servant. You name it, I've tried it. The more I served, the more aware I became of how much this big fat problem in my life was hindering me. At 274 pounds, I was physically limited in my ability to serve. In my quiet time, I began to realize that I needed to begin taking better care of myself.

My sister, Cyndi, told me about a Christian weight loss program called First Place 4 Health and suggested I consider starting a group at my church. I flat out told her that I wasn't interested. My internal battle raged on. *No, I don't want to. No, I don't have time. No, I've failed at weight loss. No, not me.* Then I thought, *Why is "no" my first response? Why is it that I follow the rules everywhere else yet when it comes to my health, I say "no"?*

The Lord is patient. He continues to work on me in my quiet time as I read my Bible and pray. Who am I to argue with the Almighty? Does he not remember my long history of weight loss failures? You name it I have done it. I am a lifetime Weight Watcher. Prescriptions worked only as long as I took them (I am part of the disaster called Fen-Phen). I have lost 40 and 50 pounds multiple times, totaling about 1,000 pounds in my lifetime. Each time, I get frustrated, quit and gain back more weight than I lost.

So whenever I sensed an internal prompting about losing weight, it was as if I'd put my fingers in my ears and scream, "La, La, La, La, La, La, La!" to drown Him out. I did not want to hear it. The longer I refused to listen, the quieter my devotion time became. I went from having a wonderful, spirit-filled quiet time to silence.

Weeks turned into months. My resistance went on for so long that I forgot why I was rebelling. I had sensed His presence in my life vibrantly for five years, and now I had experienced

months of dryness. (I hope I never go back to that place!) After many months, I searched for guides and studies to ignite my devotional time. Then one day I read a question in one of my devotionals: "What is God calling you to do today that you are not willing to do?"

"What change do you need to embrace? Say Yes!"

It felt like lightning bolts had seared through the chair in which I was sitting. I knew that God was asking me to start that weight loss group at my church. Finally, I said, "YES". I contacted my church, received permission and planned the first meeting. I knew I made the right choice when 23 women showed up.

"I'm here because God is making me," I said to the group at that first meeting. I surrendered the big, fat woman.

That began the first day of the rest of my life. My weight loss experience has been a long journey. I am blessed to be a "big loser." I emerged from it all with a life verse:

Deuteronomy 30:11
"Now what I am commanding you today,
is not too difficult or beyond your reach."

When I was struggling, or didn't think I could do it, or when I was stuck, that verse reminded me of my command: lose the weight. The Bible says it is not too difficult but it sure seemed difficult. The verse reminded me that it was not beyond my reach. I remained faithful and stuck with it.

My weight chart looks like the stock market: up, down, up, up, down, up, up, down. I've had decades of repeated weight loss, giving up, and gaining back weight. Each time I was heavier. My weight gain was a steady rise over the long haul.

First Place 4 Health challenged me to question my motive: Why did I want to lose weight? Was I trying to win the approval of others or become the healthy woman that God intended me to be? I wanted to be a healthier woman. I wanted to serve and help others every day, always. So I changed my motive and decided to do this for myself and for God, not anyone else. When I changed my motive, I was able to maintain the weight loss. By remembering my motive and my purpose, I find it easier to choose the right quality and quantity of food and find time to strengthen my body with exercise.

My final weight loss journey took four years. I reached my goal in July 2010 by losing 116 pounds. Some may think the miracle is taking the weight off but the true miracle for my life is maintaining the weight loss.

Our heart is the center of our emotional health. As an emotional eater, I used food to cope. I ate when I was happy, sad, tired, lonely, mad or even when I was bored. Food was my drug of choice. I learned new ways to cope by relying on God and embracing his love. By loving the Lord with all of my heart, I turned my emotions over to Him.

The true miracle for my life is maintaining the weight loss.

Our soul is the core of our spiritual life. My relationship with Christ is personal and interactive. I spend time every day studying the Bible, reading scripture and praying. My prayers are a two-way conversation, both asking and listening. By loving the Lord with all of my soul, I've gained astounding peace.

Our mind is the seat of our mental state. The enemy loves to lie to us by telling us we can't do something, we're not worthy or we don't know enough. By spending time in God's word, meditating and remembering scripture, I transformed my mind. By loving the Lord with all of my mind, I was able to turn over my thoughts to Him.

I look for ways to have fun with physical activity so that I remain strong.

Our body is the foundation of our physical strength. I keep a daily food diary and make healthy choices in appropriate quantities. I purposely move my body with cardio, strength and flexibility exercises. I look for ways to have fun with physical activity in my free time so that I remain strong. Sufficient rest continues to be my hardest challenge. By loving the Lord with all of my strength, I turn over my lifestyle to Him.

I learned to say "yes" and, to this day, He continues to change my life. After a 30-year highly successful career in health insurance, I took early retirement to enter the ministry. My transformation has made me lighter in body with greater stamina and clarity of mind. I now serve on staff at my church and First Place for Health. My goal is to serve all the days of the rest of my life.

What change do you need to embrace? Say Yes!

Helen Baratta *is a motivational speaker, trainer, author and coach who speaks at conferences and churches throughout the US and Canada. Her upcoming book, "Refinished and Refined", shares her journey of miraculously maintaining a 116-pound weight loss for four years and counting. She married her college sweetheart, Vince, 30 years ago and they have two grown sons. Helen loves the Lord, loves being a blessed loser and loves encouraging others to say "YES" to the Lord. Learn more at helenbaratta.net.*

Bette Novak

"There is no more brilliant light than that which follows complete darkness."

- Unknown

Chapter Fifteen
LIGHT ALWAYS FOLLOWS DARKNESS

ou are legally blind in both eyes, Bette." I was stunned as I heard these words being spoken by the eye specialist. All I could think was, *How will I be able to work?* My career as a speaker and workshop facilitator would not be possible without my vision. Forget my career - how would I take care of myself?

This news was shocking though not entirely unexpected. I'd had visual problems since I was born. In fact, I'd had no vision in my right eye for many years and doctors wanted to remove it, but I held onto the hope that one day I'd regain full sight. In recent months, I'd noticed changes, like being unable to recognize friends from across the room. Furniture and other objects that used to be clearly visible now appeared as blurry objects. While giving presentations at conferences, I feared that I might trip over the microphone cord or other wires. I couldn't clearly see the reactions from the audiences in my classroom. These symptoms caused me to feel awkward when presenting, and I often looked distracted and disorganized. I was losing my confidence as a classroom presenter. Despite these recent developments, I never expected to lose my sight or my independence; but

here I was at this eye appointment with the doctor telling me exactly that.

"It's illegal for you to drive at all," continued the doctor, "do you have a ride home?" This statement caused me to go numb. I was frightened and devastated at this news.

I had worn thick glasses since age three. Going to the eye doctor was a frequent occurrence, and my mom was diligent about taking me to the best specialists. Aside from having almost no vision in my right eye for many years, I also had glaucoma; but I never let my thick glasses or diminished vision hold me back. I sang in the choir at church and school. I was a competitive swimmer, went on to teach swimming and eventually became a life guard. I graduated from college, worked full time, traveled to almost every city in the United States, visited other countries and lived an independent life. I developed my business skills, focused on my positive attributes and never allowed my visual challenges to hold me back. That is why this new development was so devastating; it meant that I would be robbed of my independence and certainly my career.

I learned that surgery was an option but was very risky, as it could possibly restore vision in my left eye but there was a chance that I would emerge from the procedure totally blind. I struggled with this choice. The risks were dangerous and I feared losing what little vision I had left. I was terrified of living my life in entire darkness, so I decided to make the best of my situation and preserve what precious sight that remained.

At the time, my training position required travel and we lived in the suburbs with no reliable access to public transportation. My employer and coworkers generously helped me out with rides between offices, as well as to and from training engagements. My husband, Marty, became my at-home

support system and took over all the driving for errands and shopping. I was still able to work but eventually my colleagues became weary of constantly helping me.

Stress and worry made things worse. My vision began to decline quickly. Before I knew it, I was completely dependent on Marty for almost everything. I learned to count steps and feel my way around rooms but I frequently stumbled. Going out in public was always frightening. Uneven pavements, area rugs, plants, an open desk drawer or "wet floor" signs could all cause me to trip. Tasks that used to come very easy to me now took much longer. Even putting on my makeup and combing my hair became a challenge. I began to wear less makeup and cut my hair short. Dressing was also difficult since I couldn't match colors. Red looked like orange and purple looked blue. I depended on Marty to organize my clothes into matching sets. We had always enjoyed travel, but now when riding in the car I just slept because I couldn't see the sights out the window. I began to carry a magnifying glass to read when I was out shopping or at restaurants, and eventually I began to use opera glasses to navigate my way around.

At work one afternoon, I tripped and seriously hurt my right eye. What if it had been the left one? Finally, I accepted that I could no longer continue at my job but I desperately wanted to remain independent. I knew that I still had many skills and talents, including a unique ability to solve problems for organizations large and small. I was passionate about helping companies improve work processes and coaching individuals through career transitions. I decided to start my own business, LifePath Associates, LLC, and began working from home as a consultant and coach.

I was very optimistic about my new endeavor and thought that working from home would be easier and I'd have no

problem getting business. I did get some great work from a friend and former colleague but mostly I struggled. My decreased vision had taken a serious toll on my confidence. I fell several more times. I feared being left alone. Reading was becoming increasingly difficult; even with magnifiers and opera glasses, it took me longer than expected to complete assignments. As a consequence, I lost more work than I gained.

It was frustrating and I felt like a failure. Then one afternoon when I miscounted steps at home, I was forced to really face my situation. I took a very serious fall and broke my hand. This painful injury slowed my ability to work even more. I was beyond devastated. The darkness of depression now accompanied the darkness that was crowding out my sight.

In the meantime, laser surgery was quickly becoming a new standard for eye procedures and as this technique was refined, the potential for dangerous complications were significantly decreasing. I was still terrified to have eye surgery but after meeting with my doctor, we decided to take the risk and undergo two serious eye surgeries in hopes of improving my condition.

I opted to have the hardest and most dangerous surgery done first: the permanent removal of my right eye. Although I was expecting this to happen for many years, I had put it off as long as I could. This surgery was physically difficult, frightening and emotionally devastating. Even though I hadn't been able to see out of this eye for many years, I had still hoped for a recovery. The removal of this eye would end that hope forever. I finally accepted that a miracle was not going to occur. There were significant risks to this procedure but I trusted my doctor completely. My eye was removed and replaced with a coral ball. After the procedure, I had to protect my eye socket against infection. I covered it with

a realistic looking porcelain prosthetic that looks like my own eye. My recovery took about six months and I nervously prepared for the "easier" surgery: the laser removal of a serious cataract on my left eye. The eye surgeon basically removed the cataract and replaced it with an artificial lens implant. Cataract removal surgery is commonplace today but years ago it was much more dangerous. At that time, the risks involved infection, blood clots or the thing that I feared most: full loss of vision. If you have two good eyes, then this doesn't seem as risky but for me, one slight problem could leave me in darkness forever.

> *"I was terrified of living my life in darkness."*

The new laser option made this type of surgery faster and safer; it was an outpatient procedure that lasted less than two hours. When I arrived at the hospital that morning I had no right eye and the vision in my left eye was almost nonexistent. I hadn't seen colors in almost two years; everything had become gray. I had no depth perception and was literally feeling my way through life.

I had to be fully escorted and assisted through the prep process. The doctor, nurse and anesthesiologist were very kind and explained each step as they prepared for the procedure. When I woke up from the surgery, my world was completely dark. The bandage would remain on my eye for 24 hours. I was hopeful and fearful at the same time, wondering if I would have to endure this darkness for the rest of my life.

During that 24-hour period, I considered it my "rehearsal" for total and complete blindness. We would all know the results

in one day. I tried to remain calm and, fortunately, slept most of the day. I remember that Marty brought me a sandwich for dinner so I wouldn't have to use utensils. I wondered, *Will I have to learn to use a fork again?*

"Bette, I'm going to remove the bandage," my doctor said the next afternoon.

I feared the worst but had great faith in her. She gently removed the bandage, washed my eye with saline then shone a very bright light into my eye. I had experienced this light many, many times over the years. The last time my eye was examined, I barely saw the light but this time, the light was so bright it hurt! She asked me to look up, look down, look left, and look right.

Please let her see good news, please let there be no infection, I prayed silently.

When she stopped shining the light, all I could see was spots. She shut off the light and my eye began to adjust. I blinked and looked at Marty; I could see that he was smiling at me. The doctor asked me to read the eye chart across the room. I couldn't believe it! For the first time in my life, I could read every line on the chart, even without glasses! My vision in my left eye was a perfect 20/20. Everyone celebrated with me. There wasn't a dry eye in the room.

I had one good eye. My only risk now was infection. The doctor monitored me closely over the coming weeks but I recovered well. She recommended that I wear nonprescription glasses to protect my left eye, since it is the only one I have.

I felt like a newborn! On the car ride home that day I noticed that the grass was many shades of green. I read every

single road sign. The traffic lights were now three colors: red, yellow and green and not gray, gray and gray. It was a four-hour drive home and I enjoyed every moment. Most of that evening I stared into Marty's bright, blue eyes. They literally sparkled.

> *"The traffic lights were now red, yellow and green and not gray, gray and gray."*

The next day I really appreciated taking the dog for a walk and breathed in all of the beauty in our neighborhood. The world seemed so... well, colorful! Everything I looked at seemed crisp and fresh. That afternoon, I cooked, watched TV, and read. I read books, magazines, cards from friends, and even service manuals. The sights were almost magical. A month later, Marty and I went to the Department of Motor Vehicles and renewed my driver's license. I had no trouble passing the vision test. It was like a dream come true. I had my independence back once more.

Since then, I've been blessed to continue working from home and in person as a career and executive coach. I've received certifications from the Center for Credentialing and Education, and I work mainly with women who want to make career transitions, gain promotions at work or step into the encore position of their career. Working virtually, I've been able to build relationships with people from across the United States and Canada.

I understand that it's very frightening to change jobs or lose a position and face the unknown. It can be intimidating to ask

for a promotion or launch a dream business. I tell my clients that I can empathize with them. I've walked that road of facing fear, taking a risk and being uncertain about what the future holds. With confidence, I tell them something that I've learned through it all: that light always follows darkness.

Bette Z. Novak, MHRM, BCC is founder of LifePath Associates, LLC. She helps clients who want to change their careers, receive a promotion or finally leave a job they hate. Bette works with clients to develop skills that they can confidently use throughout their career. She specializes in translating, transferring and transforming her clients' expertise and experience to make them irresistible. Bette is the author of the book, "The Art of Career Survival." If you are ready to change careers, get a promotion or step into your encore position, schedule a free consultation with Bette at careeradvancementexperts.com.

Celeste LeJeune

"*Work hard, appreciate what you have, be generous, pray often.*"

- Celeste LeJeune

Chapter Sixteen

THE JANITOR'S GIRL

It's not unusual to find me speaking on behalf of a charitable cause, playing a round of golf with my husband or entertaining a large social group at my country club. My friends and colleagues today, who know me as a successful executive for a Fortune 500 corporation, might be surprised to know that for most of my younger life, I struggled as an awkward girl who never seemed to fit in.

When did I realize I was a misfit?

It might have been when I started kindergarten. My dad was the most wonderful man - a kind, gentle, caring soul and from my perspective, he mattered in the world. I felt like he had an important job that he went to each afternoon. I would admire him as he walked off to work with his lunch bag, usually a bologna and cheese sandwich. (The cheese was from our government cheese block that we received each month.) I would watch every day as he walked down the street and knew I would be asleep before he'd arrive home each night. I had quality time with my dad in the early part of each day since my mom left for her own job each morning. She would get dressed up with her hair fixed, makeup on, and

I always had the important task of making sure there were no apparent chin hairs that had popped out before she was off to catch the bus into downtown.

In those early years, my brother and sisters had the joyous responsibility of babysitting me as soon as they got home from school. They were the luckiest teenagers in the world; first school then immediately after school, babysitting their little sister. Yes, I was the youngest of five and with a significant age gap between my closest sister and me; I was what some would think of as "a mistake."

It wasn't until kindergarten that my sheltered life became disheveled as I was introduced to children who were very different than me. These children had parents who were the same age as my oldest sisters and grandparents who were the age of my parents. They didn't view my dad as the all-important person that I did either. You see, my dad was the afternoon shift custodian at the elementary school that I attended. I was delighted to see him at the end of my school day; however, the other children found amusement in making fun of me as "the janitor's girl." That label stuck with me throughout my elementary school years and it made me feel like I didn't fit in with my classmates.

My home life consisted of my brother, Michael, and three sisters - Claire, Barbara and Anita - all entertaining me until Mom got home from work. Mom was usually pretty exhausted when she returned from the city after working long hours and taking the bus each way. She was always concerned about keeping her position and never missed a day of work. I learned at a very early age that working was extremely important and holding a job meant personal sacrifices. What I didn't understand was that being a waitress at an exclusive club wasn't an executive job and that my mom worked very hard for little money. You wouldn't know

she was a waitress though because she had so much pride to be employed at this prestigious dining club. She beamed when she told stories of the clientele and her work there.

As a child, I thought that our family was well off and in some respects, we were. We shared a wealth of love and togetherness. As for material things, our home was well-kept, we always had plenty of food on the table, and our clothes were neat and clean. Those were the most important things to my parents. They never spent money on themselves and were always generous to those in need. We didn't eat out and we didn't even have a car. We took the bus downtown for any necessary shopping. We walked to church every Sunday and life was good as far as I was concerned.

My mother, who was raised during the depression, felt that as long as my clothes were clean and in good repair they were suitable for school. They were often hand-me-downs that were a little dated and never quite my size. We shopped at thrift stores and found great bargains but I was far from being fashionable. This made me an easy target for bullying and name-calling. To make matters worse, Mom still believed in cutting my hair herself. She would tell me I looked just like Olympic figure skater Dorothy Hamill as she removed the bowl from my head. The kids at school thought I looked more like the Dutch Boy on paint cans. Oh, and my front tooth had a chip in it from when I fell off my tricycle, so I was always embarrassed to show my teeth when I smiled. As if it could be any worse, I had terrible vision and the ugly glasses I wore from first grade on looked thicker than Coke bottles. I was taller than everyone else in my class so I couldn't hide either.

On top of all that, each day I would take my lunch to school; just like my dad's it consisted of a bologna sandwich with government cheese, a piece of fruit and occasionally the generic version of Vanilla Wafers. I never had to worry about

anyone wanting to steal my lunch and I always had plenty of room at my lunch table.

As I matured, I desperately wanted to fit in and have a popular circle of friends, so I decided to try out for the high school drill team. Despite the many snickers and taunting from other girls, I went to all the tryout practices. Having no social life, I had the advantage of having few distractions so I was able to practice nonstop at home. To everyone's shock, I made the drill team. I was now a pom-pom girl like all the popular girls. I was home free - or so I thought. I learned that just because you have "the title" doesn't mean you have the respect and doesn't make you fit in. This was an important life lesson. The other pom-pom girls shunned me so I hung out with the band members. Still, I enjoyed being part of the drill team and every year at tryouts, I worked harder than everyone. I discovered that the secret to achieving your goals is to work your butt off until you succeed.

I was very happy to finally be a senior so I could move on from those awkward high school days and go to college. No one in my family had done so and while my parents supported my efforts, they told me that if I wanted to attend college, I needed to pursue a scholarship. Again, I would have to work hard for what I wanted. My hard work paid off once more. I received an academic scholarship to the only college I had my heart set on, Carnegie-Mellon University. I thought to myself, "Finally, this misfit has a home!"

The joyous feeling of belonging lasted until move in day at the dorm. As I started to introduce myself to some of the students in my dorm building, I realized that most of them had better academic credentials and a lot more money than I did. I bought used books and held down two work-study jobs. At first I feared that being a "misfit" would follow me throughout my college years, but after a while, I decided

to make the most of my college experience. I made friends through study groups and social committees. I even tried out for the cheerleading squad using the same practice methods from high school and I made the varsity squad. As is turns out, those college years were great for me. I managed to thrive in new and intimidating circumstances and became a proud CMU graduate.

Me and Dad - Graduation Day at Carnegie Mellon University

I started my career with everything in mind my parents had taught me: work hard, appreciate what you have, be generous whether or not you can afford to, pray often and don't expect to be given anything. When I initially entered the workforce, I worked hard in job positions that were probably beneath me but I made the most of it and enjoyed every day. Fortunately, I gained confidence and one day joined an exceptional company that really helped me develop both professionally and personally.

While my career was moving forward, I continued to struggle in relationships. I hadn't yet learned that you cannot find fulfillment through another person; rather, it's important to first create the life you want then partner with someone who appreciates you for who you are and shares similar values.

> *"As the years went by, I realized that my life as a misfit had actually served me very well."*

As the years went by, I realized that my life as a misfit had actually served me very well. I had a great career because I knew how to dedicate myself to work. I never expected anything so whenever I received promotions and new positions within the company I humbly accepted each accolade and appreciated every new opportunity. Eventually, I became involved with charitable organizations in order to give back to others because of the opportunities that were given to me. I had a wonderful circle of friends and family so I was in a good place in my life. Then when I least expected it, I finally met the man who would become my friend, soul mate and partner. Bob, accepted me just the way I was, with all the quirkiness of my misfit life. He too was somewhat of a misfit. His love encouraged me to embrace my uniqueness, take pride in myself and accept love in a way that I hadn't before.

Currently, I am an assistant vice president for the same global company that launched my career many years ago. I value my career and continue to work hard at achieving goals. My husband Bob and I have our own family (five adopted misfit cats) and a very fulfilling life with great friends and a large extended family. I smile when people compliment me on how easily I make friends or how willing I am to make

someone new feel welcome. My life as a "misfit" is all good and I really wouldn't change anything about it. I cherish the memories of my childhood with my beloved parents who are now deceased. My siblings are still my closest friends. Now, I am proud to say I am "the janitor's girl."

Celeste LeJeune is an assistant vice president with a Fortune 500 company. She is a graduate of Carnegie-Mellon University. Celeste is a founding member of a global mentoring organization for women within her corporation. Passionate about paying it forward, Celeste is an active community volunteer with animal rescue efforts, children's charities and fundraising for nonprofit organizations. She and her husband, Bob, live in Mt. Lebanon, Pennsylvania with their five rescue cats Twinkie, Gizmo, Stuart, Elsie and Shrimpy.

Rebecca Christeson

"*Happiness is a choice, not a chase. You don't have to pursue it, just choose it!*"

— Unknown

Chapter Seventeen
BRING IT ON!

The room was filled with chatter and anticipation, as I stood waiting to be introduced to a crowd of more than 200 employees. It was my task to motivate and inspire them despite the fact that their company profits had plummeted. The organization's vice president stepped up to the podium to introduce me.

"Our speaker for today informed me that she is going to set you on fire with such passion that others will want to come and watch you burn!" he said. "Please help me welcome Rebecca Christeson!" As a motivational speaker, I'm known for my upbeat, high-energy speeches and classes. I have a passion for helping people by lifting their spirits and offering them hope. Even in my everyday life, I often strike up conversations in malls, at airports and on the street with strangers because I enjoy observing human behavior and hearing people's life stories. Others tend to confide in me and I always seek to understand and appreciate them.

I walked to the podium with a grin on my face and a prayer in my heart. As always, I wanted to connect with my audience in a meaningful way and challenge them to excel in life and

business. The expressions on those faces in the audience mirrored hundreds of people I had spoken to over the years at similar events.

I am a cheerful person by nature. I choose to be happy and teach others to do the same. I adore creating moments filled with joy and laughter. I realize that it's not easy to feel happy all the time but I know from experience that it's a choice. I offer this as an example: I've struggled with my weight the past few years and have lived with diabetes and kidney disease for many years. Right now, due to my weight, I don't fit comfortably into my favorite work clothes and I have to wear support shoes that aren't fashionable. In fact, my shoes have become quite the popular side show when I give talks. The audience often thinks that my shoes are a kick when I mention them with a big, hearty laugh. I share personal challenges such as this in a positive light in order to put people at ease. We all have hang ups, frustrations and embarrassments which are a part of our human condition.

As I stood at the podium that day I wasn't my usual high-energy self. My body felt like I'd been trudging through wet, sticky mud and my clunky diabetic shoes felt like they weighed 50 pounds each. I felt emotionally fragile, as well. You see, I had received some upsetting news earlier that week and feared that I might burst into tears before reaching the stage. My doctor had informed me that my chronic kidney disease had advanced to stage four. This caught me off guard and my mind was still reeling from the news. Since my father had died from a massive heart attack while on dialysis, I was frightened by the reality that my quality of life was about to plummet.

After learning this news, my husband, Jon, and I had a difficult appointment at the dialysis center to learn about our options for keeping me alive with kidneys that were failing. We were

stunned to learn that if I qualified for a kidney transplant, the wait could be up to 10 years. *A decade?* I thought, feeling suddenly clammy and weak. *I'll never make it that long in this condition.* The other options were equally daunting and, frankly, depressing. It all sounded like the fast track to a death sentence, a counting down of the days of my time left on earth. How long would I have some semblance of a normal life before being permanently tethered to this foreboding dialysis machine?

My emotions ranged from shock, fear and dread to pure rage and overwhelm. On the inside, I was crying out *Stop! I don't want to hear this! I can't deal with this! Why is this happening now?* Jon and I had recently become grandparents for the first time and our delightful grandson had captured my heart. You see, it had been a long time coming. Jon and I had struggled with heartbreaking infertility during the early years of our marriage. After 10 years, we adopted our son and five years later were blessed to adopt our equally precious daughter. So now, finally realizing the dream of becoming a grandmother was simply mind-blowing and glorious. I was ecstatic to be initiated into the proverbial grandparents club I'd so often heard about where you gush nonstop about every dear little thing your grandchild does. The last thing I want to be is a grandmother on dialysis. I want to run and play with my adorable grandson and watch him grow to adulthood. I want to be a strong loving influence in his life for many years to come.

Don't get me wrong, I'm grateful for the advancements in modern medicine that give me this option but I am terrified of losing my independence while being on dialysis for hours each day. This process of saving my life would no doubt adversely affect my strength, my energy and my freedom. Dialysis is not a simple process. It's not like plugging a line into a battery, recharging it and off you go. Dialysis can

have dangerous side effects, not to mention that it's time consuming and energy draining; yet it's necessary in order to replace healthy kidney function.

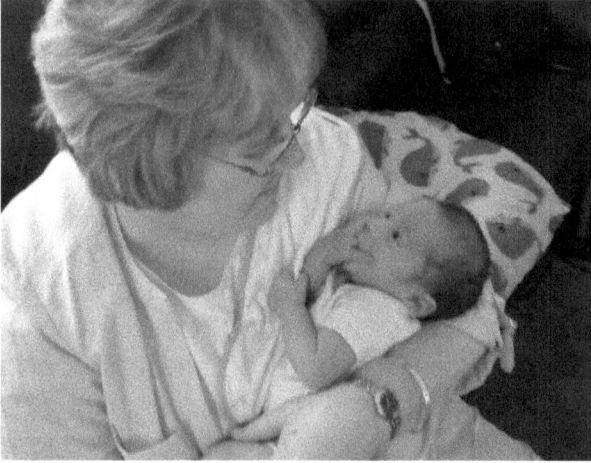

**My adorable grandson. I want to be a strong loving
influence in his life for many years to come.**

I am a proactive person by nature and choice. I do my research, seek guidance through prayer, make the necessary decisions and face head-on whatever has to be done with as much courage and grace as I can. Yet I am only human and this recent news sent me off kilter and deflated my "brave gene." I knew that everybody in my life would have to pay a price for this latest setback. Diabetes and kidney failure affects family members, friends and caregivers who tirelessly deal with the inherent daily emergencies. It's a beast of burden for everyone concerned and I felt terrible about that, as well.

All of this and more was on my mind as I stepped up to the podium that day. "Thank you for inviting me to address your group today," I began, mustering my courage and tenacity. "It is both my honor and pleasure to speak about cultivating a

more contagious, positive attitude. Are you ready to rock and roll?"

The audience cheered a collective "Yes!" and I mentally kicked into what I call the "Rebecca Zone." I put aside my personal fears and grief for the next hour and focused on giving my best to the audience. I wanted everyone to walk out of the room feeling more energized and ready to face new challenges - exactly what I was striving to do for myself. My heart was breaking but life goes on. So bring it on, I thought.

In my work as a public speaker, I encourage others to "bloom where they are planted." I've been planted in the middle of an enormous health crisis but I won't allow fear and resentment to cripple me or steal my joy. Life is a kaleidoscope of diverse situations both good and bad. The goal, as I see it, is to grasp each experience by the reins and ride it out with confidence. It helps to look at life as an extraordinary adventure.

Everyone faces challenges and how we deal with them is important; you can either eagerly accept a situation and dig deep to root yourself more firmly, or bury yourself in helplessness, shame, addiction, regret, heartbreak and confusion, with no clear direction. Actively choosing to bloom where you're planted means taking the initiative to see the positives of any situation and focusing on overcoming it. You can choose to believe in yourself and God's ability to guide you. It's possible to retain a sense of humor and move forward with optimism.

The audience was a riot to interact with; their sense of fun and apparent willingness to embrace my message, challenges and all, was thrilling. I stepped from the podium amidst laughter and a renewed sense of optimism buzzing about

the room. I remember taking a deep breath when I left the room; a feeling of renewed hope and courage permeated my very soul. I knew without doubt, regardless of the hills and valleys to come for everyone, they were going to be alright and so was I.

> *"I won't allow fear and resentment*
> *to cripple me*
> *or steal my joy."*

My goal is to make a positive impact overall, and if I have inspired but one person to want to reach a little higher and believe in their ability to improve and excel, no matter what obstacles they may face, then I am very pleased. Also, to truly believe that they deserve to experience success in reaching their varied personal and professional goals and enjoy their sense of accomplishment as a result, indeed my presentation was a success.

There is a reason and a purpose for why you are planted where you are. Have courage, you are not alone. Passionately INHALE life and EXHALE gratefulness. I believe in you and I'm expecting you to blossom.

Rebecca Christeson *is an innovative professional development training expert. She is also recognized as a successful entrepreneur, dynamic speaker and author. Her company Training With A Twist offers interactive training and workshops for organizations across the United States and Canada. Her presentations empower, inspire and educate individuals in all levels of the workforce. Rebecca's passion is to help others grow personally and professionally. Her greatest joy is being a wife, mother and grandmother. Learn more about her "Laugh Yourself Silly" series and other presentations at trainingwithatwist.com.*

Jean Haller

"Gratitude unlocks the fullness of life. It turns what we have into enough, and more. It turns denial into acceptance, chaos to order, confusion to clarity. It can turn a meal into a feast, a house into a home, a stranger into a friend. Gratitude makes sense of our past, brings peace for today and creates a vision for tomorrow."

- Melody Beattie

Chapter Eighteen

RISING FROM THE ASHES

*I*t had been a hectic couple of months. My daughter Amy's out-of-town wedding was followed by the announcement of my son's engagement and another wedding to plan within the next year. As soon as Amy's wedding was over, I began preparing my store - and myself - for the upcoming holiday rush. For a successful fourth quarter in retail, holiday preparations must begin several months in advance. For more than 20 years, I've independently owned and operated Journeys of Life, a boutique inspirational book and gift store. We are a comprehensive resource for music, handcrafted jewelry, crystals and gems, 12-step recovery books and gifts to empower people along this journey we call life.

Despite my focus on Amy's wedding earlier that year, holiday merchandise had arrived on schedule, pricing was complete and all holiday decorations were set up in a staging area in the store's basement, ready to be displayed after Thanksgiving (I never decorate for Christmas until Thanksgiving, a tradition I've kept since we first opened our doors). It felt great to be organized and ready, especially since we had dealt with a minor disaster just before the wedding: a bizarre

flash flood had filled the store's basement with more than two feet of water. Books, gifts and filing cabinets filled with paperwork were all damaged or destroyed. The paper in the file cabinets expanded with water, like a papier-mâché project gone bad. Thank goodness for business insurance; everything was replaced but it took months to clean up the resulting mess. Finally, we had things cleaned up and were ready - at least, I thought - to take on the retail holiday season.

It was about midnight on November 13, 2011 when I went to bed after an exceptionally busy day at the store. Exhausted, I was in need of a good night's sleep. Thoughts of what I would need to do in the morning occupied my mind but it wasn't hard to fall asleep, warm in my bed with my husband, Hal, and our furry Golden Retriever, Murphy. The soft pillow felt so good.

At three a.m., I was startled awake by the telephone. Hal answered it and I heard him say, "Our store?"

Hal hung up the phone, turned to me and matter-of-factly said, "The store is on fire."

We only live two blocks away so I threw on some clothes, unconcerned as to what they were, slipped into my shoes and bounded down the stairs, not waiting for Hal. I threw open the back door and could hear sirens and smell smoke. In a panic, I did something that I rarely do; I ran. I was afraid I would trip and fall, yet more afraid about what was happening at the store. I ran to the next corner and stopped, overcome by a surreal feeling. At this moment the reality of what was happening finally hit me.

Bright lights, noisy engines, firemen barking instructions, gushing water from huge hoses, and finally, the sound of

ladders being raised against the building and axes creating air holes. Several workers from the adjoining restaurants and bars who had just finished their evening shifts stood nearby watching. They told me about smelling smoke, seeing it billowing out of the vents in our ceiling and calling 911. It was somewhat comforting to have others watching all of this unfold with me. All I could do was stand and watch. I have never felt so helpless in my life.

"I never could have imagined myself sitting in a bar at 4:00 a.m. being interviewed by the arson squad."

The fire was brought under control before the second floor totally fell in on the first, thus saving the building structure but not before the entire contents were charred by flames, melted by intense heat or destroyed by smoke. All I wanted to do was go in and see what was left. Finally, the fire chief gave me permission to enter the building, but not before the arson squad interviewed me. Never in a million years could I have imagined myself sitting in a bar at 4:00 a.m. being interviewed by the arson squad. By 7:30 a.m., the frenzy was over, the fire department had gone back to their stations, the police reopened the street and I was left alone to sit in the aftermath. My entire life's work of 22 years was gone. It was almost unfathomable.

I didn't have time to wallow in self-pity, as difficult decisions needed to be made. I had built Journeys of Life from the ground up. Most of the time, I really enjoyed what I was doing. I had seen it through all stages of growth. This felt like losing a child that I had conceived, nurtured and raised just as I'd done with my own children. The store and I had survived those difficult first three years when most businesses

fail and the tumultuous teen years when I wasn't sure what the store would become. I had recently begun to contemplate retirement. Especially in recent years, the downturn in the economy, proliferation of big box stores and online competition sometimes made owning a small, independent business more frustrating than fun.

For a split second, I considered that this tragedy was my ticket out of retail. This was my lifelong passion, fulfilling a dream that grew into far more than I had ever imagined. Despite all of the wonderful rewards, there were also plenty of struggles. People do not go into this line of work for the money, certainly not by selling books. Now, I was just thoroughly exhausted. I smiled momentarily at the thought that this disaster could be my answer.

I got very quiet and knew what I was about to say to Hal.

"I'm not done yet," I said through tears that finally came. "I cannot go out this way. Not like this. I'm just not ready to be done. I hope that's okay with you".

It wasn't until I realized that Journeys of Life could be done for sure that I was able to cry. Hal wrapped his arms around me as I sobbed. Now the work would really begin.

My store manager and a dear friend had arrived at the scene for moral support. We went out for breakfast to begin planning and to make some important decisions. I have always been a person of action but I never knew the depths of my energy and passion around my business until that moment. It was less than two weeks until Thanksgiving and Small Business Saturday. I left my friends waiting at the table and walked down the street to get the phone number from the window of an empty storefront. I would have called it right then and there but it was 8:00 AM on Sunday morning. I

had been the driving force in bringing Small Business Saturday to my community. What better way to celebrate than by reopening Journeys of Life on that day? Full of drive and determination, I returned to the restaurant and sat down.

"Journeys will reopen in 10 days!" I announced, "We'll reopen in a temporary location in time for Small Business Saturday." My friends were stunned. I know for sure my husband thought I was either in shock or delusional, and shook his head in disbelief. After I filled them in on my plan to rent the empty storefront around the corner while the store was being rebuilt, we all agreed. We were off and running.

Needless to say, the next 10 days were a whirlwind of activity. I worked with a restoration company to shore up the damaged building, met with the insurance company to determine my coverage and begin the claims process, secured the new retail space, painted it and filled it with fixtures to display. Wait a minute... there was nothing to display. All contents of the building, including all my holiday merchandise, were a total loss. I knew exactly what I needed to do, something I had learned many years ago in another area of my life. I needed to ask for help. So I did just that, sounding the trumpets everywhere I could.

I notified my sales reps about what happened and my desire to be open for Small Business Saturday. They responded by bringing sample stock and sending orders from their companies. I emailed my customers telling them about the fire and our plan to rise from its ashes. A customer volunteered to design "rising phoenix" posters that we immediately displayed throughout the city. Other customers offered to help clean up and move what little was salvageable. I called my trade association and they put the word out.

I was humbled when boxes of merchandise began to arrive a few days later. My peers and colleagues who owned independent bookstores around the country donated some of their merchandise to help get me back on my feet. Vendors sent repeats of previous orders with no invoices, which represented thousands of dollars of free inventory. Cards, letters and prayers came from all corners of the country. Friends volunteered to help price merchandise and set up the "new" store. Not only did they all pitch in to get Journeys ready for Small Business Saturday, they restored my faith in humanity.

Owning a business can sometimes be a lonely journey. Having the responsibility squarely on my shoulders was sometimes daunting; however, the 22 years I had spent helping in the local community and working with businesses on a national scale was all returned to me during those 10 days. It seemed as though everyone came to my rescue. I call it karma; what goes around, comes around... and that it did.

Several days into the cleanup, two local TV stations ran stories about the fire and our will to rise again. By then, we had begun a gratitude list that hung in the temporary location with the names of everyone who helped us in some way. I saw it as a necessary part of my recovery process but the media found this intriguing. We also got coverage about our Small Business Saturday reopening. That was a day I will never forget. Hundreds of customers and friends came to support us, literally pulling us out of the ashes.

Exactly six months from the day of the fire, Journeys of Life reopened in its original location, totally renovated. Everything was new and beautiful. I cried and celebrated. I was so glad that I had not made the choice to quit.

When I reflect back on these events, I describe the fire not as a disaster but rather a blessing. When I share this with people, sometimes they are initially confused and don't understand. The store got a major do-over, something very few businesses get to enjoy in their lifespan. I was given the opportunity to put better business practices into place. I was able to refocus on what it was that Journeys had become and the direction in which it needed to go. I became a steward of the money we received, making sure that it was reinvested in the business so that Journeys would stay financially secure. Most importantly, I was given the chance to live and breathe the true mission of the store. Customers may think that Journeys of Life is in the gift-and-book business but in my heart we are in the people business. The fire brought that to light even more brightly.

**Journeys of Life reopened exactly six months after the fire.
I'm so glad I had not made the choice to quit.**

A few years ago, I was fortunate to hear spiritual teacher and bestselling author Marianne Williamson speak at a trade association breakfast. She stood on the stage, quiet for several minutes, panning the crowd and making eye contact with as many people as she could. She then thanked us for allowing her to be on that stage, giving her the gift to do what she loves, which is write books that change peoples' lives.

She spoke about her perception of stores like Journeys and said that they are more than retail establishments; they are ministries to the people they serve, and the owners and staff are the ministers. I cried as her words touched my heart. She put into words what I had known for 20-plus years: Journeys of Life began as a shop to support people in recovery and has become so much more than that.

Rising from the ashes was a community effort. Today, Journeys of Life has evolved into a safe harbor for the community, a place where we minister to those in need of support - where they've been, where they are and where they want to go. I do not take this responsibility lightly and will be forever grateful for the opportunities given to me by our customers and the community.

*Jean Haller believes that if there is a will, there's a way -
beginning with taking that first step. She is an entrepreneur
and has owned a small business for 25 years. Jean is
a community advocate and nonprofit board member,
being honored locally and nationally for those efforts. She
is contributing editor to a retail trade magazine and is a
national educator and trainer for store owners. Jean and her
husband of 38 years live in Pittsburgh. They have two grown
children. Most importantly, Jean is Morgan's grandmother, a
job she takes very seriously.*

Coulter Roberson

"Get Your Head Straight Before You Negotiate."

\- Coulter Roberson

Chapter Nineteen
LEARNING FROM MY MISTAKES

It was day two of our national conference, which was being held in my hometown. There were about 1,000 people in the room and you could feel the buzz. Everyone was cheering and clapping - except for me. I was numb. During our break, my partner in my new business - Frank, an older gentleman who was like a father figure to me - turned and asked, "What's wrong, Coulter? You don't seem like yourself today." I burst into tears and ran to the restroom. The flood gates had opened and I couldn't seem to stop crying. Finally, I pulled myself back together, took a deep breath, returned to the conference and explained to my colleague what had happened the day before.

At age 25, I had gotten married to Rusty, a man who I thought was my best friend. We were young, in love and broke. We did everything together, including partying. He liked to throw back the beer a lot more than I did. After we were married, he often drank with friends and without me. When I became pregnant with our first child, the violence began. It wasn't the punch-me, bruise-me, break-my-bones kind of violence. More than anything, it was a lot of verbal abuse. He did shape up after our first child was born for a

little while. Rusty adored our daughter and showed more love and affection to her than he did towards me.

Things became even worse when I became pregnant with our second child. Rusty's drinking and verbal insults were at an all-time high, and he was horrible towards me. I arranged to work at three different jobs that allowed me to keep my daughter with me instead of leaving her at a daycare. This time, after our son was born, things did not improve. In fact, the drinking and violence escalated. To make matters worse, I discovered that he had been having an affair with a co-worker. I began to make plans for a life without him, and that's how I found myself seeking additional income and attending this conference, where I now sat in tears.

I hadn't made a dime yet but I was building something - most of all, self-confidence. My husband did not take too kindly to my newfound self-assuredness. Nonetheless, I made arrangements to attend this conference. I asked my husband to watch the kids on day one and I asked my mom to take care of them on day two. After the first day, I came home buzzing with excitement, energy and so much self-confidence that I could finally make this business profitable and be on my way out of this horrible marriage. Rusty was not happy that he was made to babysit while I was out having fun. I went into the kitchen to cook dinner when all of a sudden I heard screaming, cursing, stomping and the kids crying. I was terrified. My husband was absolutely livid that our son caused him to spill his beer, causing him to have to go all the way out to the garage to get another one. Scared and shaking, I ran to check on both children. My one-year-old was crying with beer dripping down his head, while my three-year-old cried hysterically. By this time, Rusty had made his way out to the back yard and was throwing around patio furniture. I was terrified for all of us. Somehow I managed to remain calm. I cleaned up the children, finished making

dinner and the three of us ate together quietly, as my husband eventually left the house for the evening.

The next morning I took the children to my mom's house without a word about what happened. As I sat at the conference crying to my mentor Frank, he cautioned me, "Coulter, you can never go back to that house again. Ask your parents to let you and the kids stay with them." And that's exactly what I did. I never returned home, I moved into my parent's home with a one and three year old with nothing but the clothes on our backs.

After my divorce, I transformed into a totally different person. I felt so free to make the best decisions for my children and me. Through this sense of liberation I found my voice. When married, everything was about pleasing my husband, being there for my kids, cleaning the house and making sure the bills were paid. I lost "me" in the process. For the first time in years, I started working out, lost 50 pounds and was in the best shape of my life. I felt good about myself. What next? My career.

My company never made a profit and eventually closed, but sometimes the best doors open when you aren't looking for them. My father was a sales manager for a John Hancock Insurance Agency and he needed help with an upcoming audit. He hired me to work a few afternoons a week. I walked into an office in an industry that I knew absolutely nothing about and started auditing files to make sure the agents had neat and compliant records. After a few months of doing this, I was recruited to help interview potential agents and administer their assessment tests. This led to a full-time position. Next, I obtained my life insurance license, quit my part-time job working in a gym and traveled to college career fairs all over the state. As a recruiter I found my voice even more while interviewing recent college graduates. I was not

afraid to speak to anyone. I loved it!

We lived with my parents for three and a half years. My mom and I joke that my children had two mothers. My father started his own financial planning practice and brought me to work with him under one condition. He told me, "Pick a market, Coulter. I don't care what it is, just pick something and develop a client following." I chose women. I especially liked working with women in marriages who thought they had no way out, women who were just like I once was. I wanted to empower them to make educated, smart decisions that they could live with for the rest of their lives. I wanted to help prevent women from making poor decisions due to lack of knowledge, fear or from being bullied by their spouses.

> *"I swore to myself that*
> *I would never marry again."*

But I suppose I wasn't done learning how to protect my children and myself from a stalker (at least, that's what I tell myself). In an apparent moment of insanity, I married another aggressive, controlling and verbally abusive man. I have learned that some women tell themselves that because a man isn't hitting and causing bodily harm, she can handle it; but I knew better this second time around. I learned my lesson for good: violence should not be tolerated. I found myself filing for divorce once more.

As you can imagine, this was the most stressful time of my life. Ironically, I was finally getting along with Rusty for the first time; we were communicating more cordially so that we could protect our children from this man I was trying to escape. Six months into my divorce proceedings, Rusty was killed in a drunk-driving accident. Stunned, I wondered what could

possibly happen next.

After my second divorce, I swore to myself that I would never marry again, no matter what. My parents and friends joked that I was not even qualified to choose my own dates. I was in no hurry to date again. I waited for more than a year before even attempting it. For me, the third time was the charm! Craig was very handsome, with beautiful blue eyes and dressed impeccably from head to toe, a huge change from my previous two husbands. I was cautious but charmed. After dating for three months he told my parents that he'd found his soul mate and asked for their permission to marry me. My parents were thrilled but I wasn't so certain at first. A true gentleman, he has never been controlling or aggressive in any way. We married after dating for 18 months and had a tailgate wedding. Down south we love our college football, and his family and my family are rival fans. Our wedding was planned on the day of our school's biggest rivalry game. We had a big tailgate party, including the live mascot, a gamecock. We both finally appreciate a good relationship. Craig even adopted my children when they were 18 and 15.

Third time's a charm! Coulter and Craig's wedding celebration.

My life is very different now from that day at the national conference. Today, I help women across the United States sort through the often complex financial issues of separating assets and debt during divorce. I say, "Bring it on! The more complicated the divorce, the better!" I stand up for my clients and help them face their monsters. I find it to be very rewarding work, especially when I can empower a woman to make her own decisions about her finances - critical decisions that will affect her for the rest of her life. I have found what inspires me and gives me joy.

After nearly 10 years in business, I've helped thousands of women navigate through divorce. Through all of my experiences, I know one thing is true: There is a purpose to each experience. I have been able to help other women get through tough times of their divorce because most likely I've experienced it first hand. I tell them all the same thing. Remember, it's the life you live after divorce that counts.

Coulter Roberson is passionate about working with women going through divorce. She has personally navigated more than 100 difficult divorces, including two of her own. She works with women across the US who are frustrated and trying to get out of difficult marriages. Coulter empowers her clients to make important decisions based on education, not emotion. She has inspired thousands of women to get their heads straight before they negotiate their divorce settlements. A certified divorce financial analyst since 2006, Coulter speaks to audiences throughout the US and Canada about the topic of divorce and money. To read her blog and access some of her most popular articles, visit: splittingassets.com.

Dr. Patricia Jameson

"Let the truth of your soul shine forth."

\- Dr. Patricia Jameson

Chapter Twenty

HOLY THURSDAYS!

*H*aving survived the wrenching agony of divorce alone, I vowed that I would do my best to never let another person go through what I went through alone on their journey. In the auspicious moment when I made that pact with myself, something profound happened. I "heard" affirming voices - from angels or the Holy Spirit - that revealed the important work I would be doing in my future and inspired me to fulfill this purpose. For the first time in many months, I felt alive. I realized that my life experiences were my training ground and that I could pull from them to pave the way for my future work.

Taking my inspiration to the next level, I decided to join the movement that was breathing new life into the Catholic Church. It was the early 1980's, and new ideas and new ministries were blossoming. Parish renewal was growing and Catholic-sponsored retreats were becoming popular. Marriage and engaged encounter weekends hosted by my church were all filled to the brim. So, why not a movement to create a support group for people experiencing separation and divorce? There had never been any support system in the Catholic Church to help people negotiate this scary,

emotional-laden territory. Many Catholics still erroneously believed that they would be excommunicated from the church if they divorced. I found it to be very sad that people who felt they had failed at marriage were, at the same time, feeling unwelcomed and unloved by their church. It certainly didn't help that the parish community judged and gossiped about those who were experiencing divorce. I definitely needed to put an "X" through this "Scarlet Letter" situation.

I took the initiative and began placing announcements in church bulletins. Nearly 100 people attended the first meeting. The effort caught on and soon became known as HEART, or "Helping Each other Accept change, Resume life and Trust again." The members came up with that name and took ownership. Soon, groups were meeting weekly and the agenda was created from the needs and desires of the members. We did not limit our groups to just Catholics; all were invited to participate. We shared our stories, healed together, grew together and learned to trust again.

Word of our efforts spread. Soon I began hearing from other people interested in starting self-help support groups in their churches. Over the next four years, support groups for divorced and separated individuals sprung up everywhere. I was invited by the Pittsburgh Diocese to be a part of their new Family Life initiative and to help them create an outreach program. I was amazed, pleased and humbled to know that I'd lit a flame of change that was now burning bright. The voice of the Holy Spirit kept me moving and I found myself being involved with even more self-help group creators. Together, we ignited a community wide Self-Help Group Network. The vision that was foretold to me was coming true.

These HEART meetings sprang up everywhere, and continued for more than eight years. I thought that things were going great. Life sometimes works like that; you are in the abyss,

scrambling and scraping your way to the surface, then you take a breath, get creative, start something new and are feeling really great... and wham!... something comes out of the blue and blows you away. Sometimes when one's originality starts to shine, it reminds others of the how they let their light go out, and jealousy rears its ugly head in order to snuff out any other light source. Well, in this case, the forces of the patriarchal church announced that we could no longer meet on church property - most likely because our meetings were open to all denominations and we did not fully embrace the "annulment process for all" Catholic dictum. I was curtly informed that the group would either be taken over by priestly leadership or have to be dissolved, and that I should hand over the member list immediately.

Remembering my own lonely experience in the midst of divorce and the higher calling that inspired me, I summoned my inner "wild woman" and, along with the other group members, offered the patriarchy a resounding "No way!" Feeling empowered, we simply found another meeting place at the local YMCA.

With the encouragement of two very special friends, I made my way back to school to complete my undergraduate degree. I decided upon a dual major in theology and psychology and thought I could now get paid for my work in the Church and generate a family income. My real life angels were unknowingly helping me to continue to pave the way for my future work.

I discovered that the college I'd chosen to attend had a historical mission to "educate women in a process of self-directed, lifelong learning, freeing them to think clearly and creatively, to discover, challenge, affirm cultural values... and to render competent compassionate service." As I read this information, I knew that I was exactly where I was meant to

be. I'd already conquered the thinking creatively part; now it was time to learn more about "challenging cultural values." From deep within I felt a pulsing, heartfelt desire to grow, learn and discover the "more-to-it" of life. I burned hot with that passion. In my 'more-to-it' moment, I realized how so many were taught to accept suffering and humbly bear their cross. None of that made any sense to me. What about learning how to not create the suffering in the first place? What about gathering up all the crosses, making a beautiful bonfire and inviting the bearers over to roast marshmallows and eat s'mores?

"I summoned my inner wild woman."

Through my theology and psychology coursework and the college's emphasis on social justice my thoughts about oppression were confirmed. As fate would have it, during my senior year, a compelling and life changing opportunity landed in my lap. I received a call from my friend, Madeline, asking if I had heard about the bishop's memorandum forbidding women from participating in the Holy Thursday foot washing ritual. In sending that memo, the bishop was trying to be efficient, giving churches and religious communities a heads up for the upcoming Easter season. At the very least, Madeline and I thought we should gather a few people together to chat about this and formulate a response. We quickly devised a plan. Madeline called her friends and I called mine, and we scheduled a local meeting. My voices urged me to alert the media and, as a result, close to 400 people attended, including local and national media.

Noted liberation theologian Matthew Fox taught me that prayer was meant to be an action, not something to keep in the privacy of my heart. He called it "radical prayer" and showed that it changes lives, shifts paradigms, frees people

from oppression and radically changes the way we live. I realized that radical prayer was a tool that could help me on my mission to end private suffering and help change the world. Those voices no longer need to only be in my head; they could join with the voices of all the people who came that eventful night. Finally, we could all be heard.

"The mission spread like wildfire."

The Holy Thursday rally attracted a diverse group, including social justice priests, radical religious women, married clergy, folks advocating for women priests, gays and lesbians, and the "let's just go and find out what this is all about" people. At the opening of the meeting, Madeline and I looked at each other with no idea how to properly begin. Our radical prayer began as everyone voiced their outrage and decided on a plan of action. We ended the evening by joining together in singing "One Bread, One Body." Madeline and I washed the hands of everyone in attendance as a symbolic gesture of unity. Our work was cut out for us in the weeks ahead.

The mission spread like wildfire. Our story was all over the newspapers, and both local and national broadcast media ran stories and interviews on an ongoing basis. Some Catholic women decided to go on strike; they stopped teaching CCD and housecleaning for priests. Others wanted to talk with the bishop and learn his motives. Some wanted to be media liaisons. Others wanted to organize participant information or plan protests. And still others wanted to plan a special Holy Thursday celebration that included women. There were so many voices, so many ideas, so much energy, and so much hope for change. We had opened Pandora's Box and what resounded most loudly for me in the midst of it all was the long suffering being expressed by so many people who had quietly endured the pain of marginalization.

In 1986, Madeline and I changed Holy Thursday foot washing, starting in our community. From there, we changed the Catholic Church and impacted women worldwide. These days, hardly anyone remembers when women were *not* included in this sacred ritual but we have all the pictures and newspaper clippings to prove it. This, we learned, is the business of radical prayer - turning inspiration into action.

Since then, I've earned a doctorate degree and have become a faculty member at my college. In 1996, I founded the Aletheia Center for Healing and Empowerment, a counseling center for individuals, couples and families. In Greek mythology, Aletheia means revealing the truth. The center is dedicated to alleviating suffering, promoting healing, encouraging growth, enlivening the passion of the human heart and enabling people to realize their dreams.

Helping individuals move from oppression to liberation has become my life's work. It is the focus of my counseling practice and integral to all my courses and, most especially, the groups I facilitate. You see, for the past 16 years, I have been gathering all those who have suffered, been marginalized and carried crosses at the hands of oppressive people. And every Thursday night I 'wash' their feet as we gather around the collective fire to share our stories, heal and grow together and eat s'mores.

Dr. Patricia Jameson is a counselor, educator, author and advocate. She started the Aletheia Center for Healing and Empowerment 20 years ago as a professional counseling center embracing a holistic approach to healing and empowerment of mind, body and spirit. In addition to her client work, she facilitates a weekly empowerment group and offers specialized workshops and trainings. As full-time faculty at Carlow University, Dr. Pat teaches psychology and women's studies courses in the School for Social Change. She has worked in a variety of settings helping to create growth-fostering communities. Learn more at drpatjameson.com.

Terry Natale Ranieri

"Live simply, so others may simply live."

\- Mother Theresa

Chapter Twenty-One
LIFE IS A JOURNEY OF LESSONS

My earliest recollections in life were when I was five years old, living with my parents, Raffaela Della Vecchia and Michelle Natale, my brother Mario and my two sisters, Filomena and Giovanna. Our home was a two-room house on a small farm in the region of Campania, Italy. It was 1955 and times were very difficult for my family and our war torn country. My father took whatever work he could find and my mother worked in the fields to grow our food. I remember hearing my parents crying sometimes, fearful that we would not have enough to eat. Filomena and Mario went to school during the day and Giovanna stayed with my mother. I spent my days wandering in the beautiful hillsides around our home.

My love for the freedom of being outdoors remains with me today. I can vividly recall the tastes of the figs and green plums that grew in our gardens, and the exotic scent of wild chamomile. Each afternoon, I walked through these fields to wait by a big old tree for Filomena to return from school. She and I were very close. Since our mother spent so much time working in the fields with Mario, Filomena was responsible for me and Giovanna after school. My first memory of being

truly loved and cherished came from Filomena. She was, at 10 years old, the kindest and most giving little girl and my best friend in the world.

Filomena became seriously ill after being vaccinated in school. She was in bed for a month, and I stayed by her side and held her hand every day. Even when she was so very sick, she encouraged me and did not want me to worry. My parents used every possible resource they could find and were desperately trying to help Filomena get well. One afternoon, she looked into my eyes and said that she could not stay with me any longer. She told me that angels were coming for her and that I needed to be brave and good for my parents, and take care of little Giovanna. She wanted me to have all her belongings, especially her brand new shoes. That evening my sister entered heaven and my life as a child ended. My heart was broken and the sadness within me was so powerful and immense that it has remained with me for my entire life. For a long time after we lost Filomena, I would go to the old tree and wait for her. I prayed for the angels to bring her back to me.

Throughout my life I've felt something missing, a piece of me lost. At the same time, I know that she's been my guardian angel, guiding me through the journey of my life and inspiring me during tough times. No matter how difficult the challenges have been, I still see her smile and feel her beautiful spirit. During the 1950's, Italy was in economic turmoil. Devastated at the loss of their precious daughter and struggling to support us, my parents felt that they needed a new start. My mother's father was a U.S. citizen and had family living in the states. Determined to create a better life for our family, my mom bravely left Italy. She was 32 years old and eight months pregnant when she boarded a ship alone and headed to America. She stayed with family and one month later gave birth to my brother, Anthony. Mom found

a job in a tailor shop, while the rest of us remained behind in Italy. Dad worked doubly hard at his job and on our small farm. I was responsible for Giovanna and when I felt sad and lonely I remembered Filomena's words and imagined that she and the angels were watching over us.

Mom worked hard, established residency and, within a year, raised enough money to bring all of us to America. She wrote to us often and told us that she cried every night; she missed us but promised that our new life would be much better. I learned from my mother how to be brave, strong and courageous, and I looked at this voyage as an exciting (though frightening) adventure. Our little village in Italy was very remote. We had no electricity or indoor plumbing. I never could have imagined myself flying in the air to a faraway city in a giant machine. It was October 1958. I was eight years old and Giovanna was five. We held hands the entire flight. My family rejoiced when we landed at the airport in New York City. Soon we would be reunited with Mom. I can still remember walking through the airport and seeing a mysterious woman with flowing red hair and bright red lipstick coming my way. It was my beautiful mother. *Wow! America is different!* In Italy, Mom had looked years older, with heavy dark clothing and her hair severely pulled back in a bun. Here, she was youthful, energetic and filled with hope.

That first Christmas was a struggle for my parents. They could not afford gifts for us and instead of a traditional dinner, we had spaghetti with garlic, olive oil and one can of anchovies. Mom had to cook the sauce first and then the spaghetti because we only had one pot. That Christmas eve, we sat in our small rented house feeling safe and grateful but also sad due to leaving our extended family and customs in Italy. A knock on the door changed everything. Jolly Uncle Tony was there, overflowing with dolls, bikes, delicious specialty foods and a used television. My parents cried with joy as we all felt

the spirit of Santa Claus coming to our home. I remembered Filomena and imagined her celebrating in heaven. Our future Christmas celebrations were abundant but that first Christmas in America was a special memory for all of us.

"Jolly Uncle Tony came with dolls, bikes, food and a used television."

My Uncle Tony taught me how to be kind, how to spread hope and joy, and how small deeds make a big difference. Life at home was happy but school was very difficult for me.

I was teased relentlessly about my accent and the way I looked. My mother would tell me every day, "Theresa, don't let those children affect you! When they are mean to you, just smile, because someday you will rise above them. You need to work hard and get a good education." Mom was right but still, I hated being the poor girl from Italy. I can still remember the times that I had to sit in class alone because we could not afford 25 cents to attend glee club with the other children. Fortunately, in fifth grade I had a wonderful teacher, Mrs. Devlin, who taught me to never give up. She'd stay after school to tutor me in reading and English. At the end of that school year, I was recognized as the most improved reader and was awarded a figurine of the Blessed Mother with baby Jesus. I still have that statue in my china closet.

By the time I reached high school, I had become a confident young woman. It was a larger school where no one knew me as an immigrant. I worked very hard and achieved high honors all four years. I became a student officer and was recognized for my loyalty and school spirit. I can still see my parents in the audience smiling with pride as they watched

their first daughter graduate. What they taught me had paid off; I worked hard and was rewarded for it.

I could not afford to attend college full time so I went to work at the University of Pennsylvania and took college courses at night. I started out as a secretary but had bigger goals. During the early 1970's, the workplace was very different for women than it is today. Most women worked in clerical or support positions. I worked hard, put in extra hours, found mentors and proved myself. By the age of 25, I had my own secretary and an office overlooking the city. As a fundraising professional for the university, I was a woman in a leadership position and my advancement gave the women in the office pool inspiration that they could also be promoted. I'm proud that I helped put a small chip in the glass ceiling. Every time I see the movie *Working Girl*, I reflect on that special accomplishment with a smile.

My siblings and I have a very strong connection; they are my past and future. My parents taught us to stay together and support and love each other unconditionally. Mario was 15 when we arrived in the United States. He went to work in a brush factory to financially help the family. He was - and still is - the family protector, driver and humorist. No matter what came his way, he took it in stride with a smile, a joke, a kind heart and positive attitude. Mario worked hard, raised a great family and achieved the American dream. I always feel happy and safe when I am with my big brother.

Giovanna (we call her Joe) will always have a piece of my heart and I thank God every day for her love and support. We have never stopped holding each other's hands throughout our life experiences. As children, I was her protector; today, she is one of my heroes. When we arrived in the United States we were blessed to meet our youngest brother, Anthony. Giovanna and I adored him and still think of him as our baby,

but today he is a fine, hardworking, successful man who we are proud to have as a brother and friend.

My father was always a joyous man with a smile on his face and a twinkle in his eye. Dad worked for many years for a utility company and eventually became a professional gardener at the University of Pennsylvania, a job that gave him great pride and joy. One of the special traits of my father was always saying "thank you" and having gratitude for everything and everyone that came to his life. Daddy taught me to always show gratitude to God, and appreciate family, friends and strangers who crossed my path.

Filomena's spirit has been with me through my entire life, in good times and bad. I know for certain that she is in heaven with my parents today. Knowing her, then losing her, taught me how to be a compassionate and caring woman, always sensitive to others who are experiencing loss or challenges. I've been truly blessed by my family and have received a great deal of strength from each of them.

In 2011, I was diagnosed with stage 3 colon rectal cancer. With the devotion of my husband, Nick, my sons, Nick Jr. and Rob, daughter in-law Jamie, and the support of my family and friends, I fought the disease with a "can do" attitude. It was a challenging time, with two operations, chemotherapy and radiation treatments. I learned a lot about life during this difficult experience. Most importantly, I discovered that I no longer need to seek the missing piece of my life. I found redemption.

My core belief is that our experiences shape who we are. We need others to help us overcome the difficulties of life and go on to fulfill our own unique purpose. No matter what happens in life, work hard, believe in yourself, pray, give and accept help from others, and do what you need to do. The

death of a loved one, poverty, discrimination, loss, anger, disappointment and even cancer is all just part of life's journey and its inherent lessons. In fact, sometimes these challenges can become the beginning of a new and more appreciated life.

Terry Natale Ranieri *is a devoted mom, nonni, wife, sister, daughter, career woman, friend, cancer survivor and inspirational speaker. She's enjoyed a successful professional career and was one of the first women to chip through the glass ceiling. Her passion is to help all women recognize that life challenges can also become life lessons. Terry and her husband Nick live and work in Palm Coast, Florida. She's the author of the upcoming book "The Journey of Living Life."*

Mary Frances Gargotta

"None of us knows how long we have to live. Don't live an unfulfilled life."

- Fran Gargotta

Chapter Twenty-Two
THE GAME CHANGER

*I*n 2011, I was a vital and dynamic businesswoman. Fiercely independent with an abundance of energy, I could run circles around most people, even those half my age, and I could do so wearing high heels. I took pride in being productive and accomplished. I truly enjoyed my work as an executive and arrived in the office each day by 7 a.m. My calendar was always filled with business, alumni, community, board obligations and church activities, so I was rarely home until 10 p.m. I was in excellent physical health, ate well, went to Pilates classes and worked out six days a week. I loved my life but somewhere deep inside, I wondered if I should be doing something different with my life - if maybe I had a deeper purpose to fulfill - but my busy life kept those thoughts from surfacing too often.

In the spring of that year, at the urging of one of my co-workers, I phoned my doctor. I had been having serious headaches and was taking a lot of over-the-counter pain relievers. When I told my physician of my symptoms, he was very concerned.

"Fran, in all the years I've known you, you've never complained

of headaches," he said. "Let's send you right to the neurologist for some tests - and, Fran, don't put this off."

I learned that I had a very large brain aneurism and the neurologist advised me to have immediate surgery; but I had a lot of things on my calendar and Easter was coming. The specialist explained that most likely this aneurism had been with me for my entire life, so I thought a few more weeks wouldn't hurt. I spent the next month or so getting ready to take a seven-week leave, the expected time for recovery. I busied myself in preparations, as if I was going on vacation. I completed all the work projects that I could, trained my team to manage my most important responsibilities, and delegated my civic obligations to others. At home in the evenings, I planned out all of the home projects that I could complete while recuperating.

The surgeons told me that I had nothing to worry about; they were fully confident that after surgery I would be even better than I was now. Oddly, I was looking forward to the time off. The plan was to be in the hospital about four to six days after the surgery then spend the next several weeks resting, relaxing, reading and decorating. I even pictured myself doing some writing, which had always been a goal of mine.

As I was being prepped for surgery, the surgical team assured me once more that everything would go well. My friends and family were there to wish me well, and the last thing I remember was being wheeled into the operating room, looking forward to my seven weeks off.

And then I woke up. I wasn't myself, at all. I learned later that there were complications during surgery and that I'd experienced a stroke. I felt very dazed and light, as though half of my body was missing. I tried to speak but could not. Extremely fatigued, I had no strength at all. The medical staff

became concerned about my condition after surgery, and when we discovered that I did not have the ability to swallow they became alarmed. Things went from bad to worse while in the hospital. All of my major systems began to shut down and I was placed in quarantine on three occasions. The physicians were puzzled by my condition. The four-to-six day hospital stay turned into three weeks. At discharge, I was still unable to walk or eat, and was attached to a feeding tube.

My sister was kind enough to let me stay with her while recovering. I remained in her constant care for the next several months, as I worked with therapists to learn to walk, swallow, and regain my independence. This was not the recovery that I had planned. Physical therapists worked with me several times a week to help me regain my strength and eventually move from a wheelchair to a walker, and many months later to a cane.

Speech therapists helped me to regain my ability to swallow but it took more than three months before I was disconnected from the feeding tube. I'll never forget my first meal; it was a small piece of turkey on Thanksgiving Day, almost six months after my surgery. My family celebrated around me.

I was very blessed to have the support of family and friends and while I feared not being able to return to work, my team there really rallied and managed things exceptionally well. Company owners encouraged me to get better and come back when I could.

Meanwhile, my doctors and therapists continued to be mystified at my condition. Essentially, I was told "Fran, this is as good as it is ever going to be." Although I had learned to eat (barely) and walk again, I was very fragile and was unable to leave my home without assistance; to be honest, I preferred to stay there and be a hermit.

I wondered, during this dark time, if this was God punishing me for something, or retribution for bad choices I'd made in a previous life. My medical team had nothing more to offer but I was not ready to accept this situation as permanent. I wasn't willing to live the rest of my life feeling fatigued, weak, vulnerable and dependent on others.

Frustrated, I began to explore the world of alternative/complimentary medicine. The first ray of hope came from my chiropractor, Dr. Bob Yakovac. I had seen him regularly when I was an active, energetic person who exercised regularly and slept very little. He was unaware of my surgery and post-op complications, so when I arrived at his office leaning on a cane, he was stunned. That day, Dr. Bob spent so much time with me that he ran late the rest of the day. He kindly volunteered to manage my case and immediately arranged for me to see an acupuncturist to begin regaining my strength and a conditioning coach to regain my balance.

Finally, my journey to wellness had begun. My case was complicated and Dr. Bob monitored my recovery process, even encouraging me to take voice lessons to improve my damaged vocal chords. Dr. Bob helped me to understand how my brain and body's energy systems work in harmony. With my energy levels slowly returning, I began to seek even more healing modalities. I came to rely on Reiki, meditation, nutritional counseling, body/energy work, water therapy, scalp acupuncture and an exercise coach.

As my body began to heal, I also benefited greatly from the spiritual support of my friends. Many people from dozens of religious denominations were praying for me; my own church community was so very supportive. Members of my congregation visited often, took me shopping and out to restaurants (even though I couldn't eat) just to get me out of the house. They brought gifts and sent cards, letters and

flowers. One family brought me communion every week, and another friend brought a priest from another church to anoint my throat. My church family went out of their way to assist me during the lowest time of my life and, in the process, taught me that it's okay to rely on others.

> *"I took a leap of faith*
> *and began to write.*
> *The words just flowed."*

As I continued my recovery process, I was gradually able to begin to work remotely. While I was hopeful that a full recovery was possible, I couldn't help but wonder if I might be avoiding some lesson that I was meant to learn through all of this. Did I have a greater purpose in life? Had I been avoiding it with my busy and hectic lifestyle? I certainly had been successful in each endeavor, personal and professional, but was I supposed to do something more? I'd always felt that I had a higher calling but never took the time to explore the possibilities. Was this experience urging me down a new path? Was God telling me that He had a different plan for me? Was this His idea of an intervention?

Before my surgery, I had yearnings to become an author and a speaker. I had even attended classes to become a certified coach but my busy life got in the way of fulfilling those desires. Was it now time to do so? I felt simultaneously nervous and excited by the notion yet as I began to tentatively reconnect with professionals in my community about this, I received validation. A lot of influential people began to cross my path - spiritual teachers, successful coaches and authors. With encouragement from these individuals, I took a leap of faith: I started my own coaching company and began to write on a regular basis. What I

discovered is that I have a lot to say. The words just flowed out of me.

Looking back, my health crisis was a game changer. Today, I have the opportunity to inspire and encourage others in a way that I was never able to before. Most people make radical changes in their lives because they are unhappy or unfulfilled. I needed a little nudge - no, a big nudge - to step onto the right path. It's been a very long journey but in a strange way, very worthwhile. Through adversity, I learned what I could really achieve.

These days, my road to recovery is not as steep as it has been. In some ways, life is not the same as it was before the surgery, and I'm not sure that I'll ever wear high heels again. Still, I'm on the right path and have plenty of guidance and support around me. My climb to success is not the one I had initially planned but somehow, this journey is even sweeter.

Fran Gargotta is a game-changing leadership coach who works with leaders to be the best they can be. Fran's clients understand that in order to be profitable and productive, teams must overcome communication, technology, culture and collaboration challenges. She's taught leadership, management, team building and effective communications for a number of companies and nonprofit organizations. Fran is certified by the International Coach Federation (ICF) as a Professional Certified Coach. She received her bachelor's degree from the University of Pittsburgh and her master's degree from Carnegie Mellon University. Learn more at Game-ChangingLeadership.com.

Joyce D. Barton

"*The ideal healthcare system needs to start with each of us making healthy food and lifestyle choices.*"

\- Joyce D. Barton

Chapter Twenty-Three
FOOD WITH JOY - A FAMILY'S TALE OF THE POWER OF FOOD

I watched my mother be beaten by an agonizing battle with brain cancer. No one ever expected to lose her to such a devastating disease. When she died, we all felt lost without her. Four years later, my younger sister, the baby of the family, was diagnosed with breast cancer. She loved life and wanted so much to live.

As I stood at the foot of Lynda's hospital bed with the rest of the family, watching her suffer and ultimately take her last breath, I remember thinking, *how can this be happening again!?* Then the unthinkable happened. Three weeks later, the day before Lynda would have celebrated her 49th birthday, her daughter was tragically killed in a horrific car accident. I was numb. There was an overwhelming sense of helplessness that I did not know how to handle. To make matters worse, my marriage of 23 years was falling apart. The stress was unbearable. It became clear to me that I had to take control of my life. Two years later, I found myself behind the wheel of a box truck, moving my stuff to Florida. As I drove the 950 mile trip, I thought about life, how it can change in the blink of an eye and the things that affect it.

I'm blessed to still have Dad in my life. I receive so much strength, joy and inspiration from him. He always made me feel like I could do anything. To this day, I continue to learn from his vast life experiences. Over the years he poured his heart into building businesses. Dad worked a variety of businesses throughout his life and didn't retire until he was 83. Ten years later, he said, "I'm bored. I think I'm going to open up a used car lot." And he did.

"My dad taught me the joys of longevity and eating well."

However, the most important thing to him has always been his health. Eating a natural diet is top on his priority list. At 97 years old, he looks and acts like a man half his age. He has sparkling blue eyes, a bright smile and smooth, wrinkle-free skin. Most people think my dad is just lucky or must have "good genes" because he's lived such a long life and hasn't been really sick or suffered with any disease. He says luck has nothing to do with it. Dad set a goal many years ago to live to be 100. He makes a conscious effort to give his body wholesome, natural foods - mostly fruits, nuts and vegetables - to keep it healthy. He says it's his form of health insurance. As a result of that principle, my dad is not lying in a nursing home waiting to die. He enjoys each day, living life fully.

Not too many fathers care about the importance of a natural diet, at least not back in the 1950's and '60's when I was growing up. I have fond memories of our family kitchen when I was a young girl. Dad encouraged us to enjoy a bounty of colorful whole foods. He was definitely ahead of his time! Dad knew that there was a direct connection between eating simple, whole foods and a having a disease-free life. During an era when the country was in a craze over canned ham,

packaged snacks and pseudo-cheese that came from a spray can, my family snacked on apples and avocados. He made it fun! I loved helping him grind up raw cashews to make fresh nut butter and excitedly watched him crack open a coconut to get to the sweet juice and meat inside.

Most of our meals were simple foods like bananas and grapefruits for breakfast, cucumber sandwiches for lunch and a variety of home cooked vegetables for dinner. We weren't necessarily vegetarians but I don't remember meat being the center of any meal. Other than our overtly natural diet, my family lived a pretty typical life. My three sisters and I grew up just like everyone else in our neighborhood. We had a single family home in the suburbs, snazzy Easter outfits, new cars and even enjoyed fun summer vacations at the beach.

Dad has always been a very driven man and worked very hard to provide his family with a good life. While my friends' fathers went to work in their nine-to-five jobs each day, my dad was always in business for himself. His first company was Barton Tea & Coffee Company that he started in the 1940's. After serving in the US Navy during WWII, Dad went door-to-door using his own delivery truck. That company expanded to four delivery trucks with several employees. As the years went on, he progressed into other businesses, eventually owning four restaurants, two mobile home parks and, today, a car dealership.

Being different from everyone else was really tough for my mother. That crazy natural lifestyle just wasn't working for her. When I was 10, she took us away, divorced my dad and got remarried. Suddenly, there were no more coconuts and avocados. We found ourselves eating the Standard American Diet (S.A.D.). Mum seemed to be relieved when we ate the sugar-laden boxed cereals that my step-father approved of. Looking back now, I can see how these

choices were pivotal in all of our lives.

The divorce was tough for my dad. He adored my sisters and me. Even though he was distressed after the divorce, he remarried too and continued to build his business empire. And always, always, always at the core of his beliefs was living a natural and healthy lifestyle.

Me and my inspiration--Dad at age 97

When I graduated from high school, Dad didn't send me to college. Instead, he brought me into his world again... the world of the restaurant business. He taught me that in order to understand the business I had to learn everything about it, from peeling potatoes in the basement to payroll processing in the office. I learned it inside out, and with more than 100 employees, it was quite a task. Work became my life. We traveled to big cities for the restaurant shows where I was exposed to the industry on a much larger scale. I learned to negotiate deals, create new menu ideas and start employee training programs. I worked alongside my father for over 20 years, learning everything from human relations to business development to culinary arts. He taught me a very strong

work ethic. I was consumed with work and loved every minute of it.

Dad knew that our part of the world wasn't ready for a menu with fruits, nuts and veggies. In our restaurant, we served typical home-style foods like pancakes and eggs, hamburgers and French fries, Broasted chicken, stuffed pork chops and lots of pies, cakes and ice cream. You'd never find Dad eating like that though; our office always smelled like a fruit farm. The trash can was full of banana peels, grapefruit skins and apple cores. Even though I enjoyed fresh and healthy foods, I have to admit that I wasn't fully committed to his lifestyle back then. I just didn't think it was that important. I felt invincible to the inherent dangers of what Dad called poor food choices. We all rebelled from one degree to another by making unhealthy choices. Some of those choices had profound effects on our entire family.

I learned over the years that our bodies need healthy foods, healthy relationships and healthy environments. My beautiful mother died from a brain tumor at age 73. My mother and father were not married when she died, but he was there to hold her hand as she took her last breath. Mum had given little regard to eating healthy foods after the divorce. She ended up in an unhappy marriage filled with stress and negativity. I watched her struggle at the end, wanting to live a happy life but caught in a situation that came from poor choices.

My sister Lynda was the most stubborn one in the family when it came to following Dad's advice on nutrition. I suspect that she resented Dad's natural lifestyle because she associated it with the divorce. When Lynda was diagnosed with stage 3 breast cancer, she kept the cancer a secret from him for a long time. She refused to let Dad impose his beliefs about natural living on her because she felt they were too extreme.

The doctors offered little hope and didn't expect her to live. She endured a lumpectomy, chemotherapy and radiation. Three years later, she needed additional surgery on her liver, where the cancer ultimately metastasized. That surgery resulted in an open wound in her side that never healed. Her final demise was from a massive heart attack, but even then she held on for three more days. She desperately wanted to live to see her children achieve their goals, but her body couldn't take any more. The onslaught of chemotherapy, surgery and wound treatments was too much stress, both mentally and physically. I wondered, *What is more extreme: Dad's lifestyle or a losing battle with cancer?*

It was hard to lose Lynda at such a young age. Dad so wanted to help her. He knew how... if she would have only listened.

It's hard to say how things would have turned out if Mum and Lynda had followed Dad's advice. But, I do believe the closer you eat in accordance with nature, the more likely your body will thrive and not just survive, or worse yet... cease. The simple fact is we only have one life to live. It only makes sense to give our bodies the best opportunity to provide us with a long and healthy life through optimal nutrition and loving relationships. My heart aches every day for the loss I have endured and the suffering that people go through on a regular basis in our country. I look at Dad with such admiration and respect that he wants to help people realize that the answer lies within the power of our own body to heal itself, if we would only give it what it needs.

We all hope that one day cancer will be a thing of the past but until then, we cannot rely on a cure; we must focus on prevention. That is why I decided to pour my heart and soul into helping people make the transition to a healthier lifestyle. After I moved to Florida, I became certified as a holistic

health coach through the Institute of Integrative Nutrition, where I learned from the world's leading health experts.

Now, I am 57 years old and I look and feel better than I did when I was 35. I have taken the inspiration that I received from my father to live a healthy life and coupled it with my own experiences and the certification training that I received. I know now that Dad has been right all along: Food is a very powerful force that should be understood and respected, as well as enjoyed. That is why when I founded my company in 2012, I decided to name it Food With Joy. I believe the process of getting healthy can be a happy one, not a struggle or punishment.

Everyone knows that they should make better lifestyle choices but that's not always easy in today's world. As my clients' wellness partner, I guide individuals through the changes they need to make and hold them accountable to the process with love and support.

My dad taught me the joys of longevity and eating well. My family taught me to appreciate how precious life is and why we need to enjoy every moment. I know for sure that getting healthy is not only fun, it's also the most important gift you can give to yourself and your loved ones.

Joyce D. Barton is a certified holistic health coach and the founder of Food With Joy, LLC. She received her training from the Institute of Integrative Nutrition, where she learned from the world's leading health experts. Joyce works with busy professionals who want to look good, feel good and have more energy. She takes the drudgery out of getting healthy and makes it exciting and fun. Her coaching programs are available in person or online at foodwithjoy.com.

Deanna DiGioia

"*I'm not afraid anymore. I am healing. I am empowered.*"
- Deanna DiGioia

Chapter Twenty-Four
REJOICE IN YOUR VOICE

I'm in the battle of my life advocating for my children and myself since I left my marriage almost three years ago. I learned quickly that the family division of the law is flawed. This system (like my marriage) operates in a "power over" way, where one person or group of people has perceived power over another. In such a reality, there is an oppressor and a victim. Both sides have to agree to live this way in order for it to work. Fear becomes the driving force. How do I function in this fear-based world and do the right thing for my family? Healing and advocacy do not have a place in this world. I'm not afraid anymore. I am healing. I am empowered.

My first experiences in the legal system are a blur to me now. Like other divorce cases, ours was assigned to a judge and the fate of our family rested in her hands. Judges hold the power to make decisions that may or may not have a family's best interests at heart. My initiation into the system was being told that in order to file papers for divorce, either my husband or myself would have to leave our residence. It took years for me to gather the courage to even think about leaving, even though my spouse was abusive. After all, I had two

small children to consider. I had never filed a Protection From Abuse order or a police report of any kind, since I thought that these options could be used to protect myself only when I was ready to leave the marriage. I rationalized that filing charges against my spouse - then having to continue living under the same roof with him - could pose additional problems. How could a strong, smart, successful woman like me wind up with no identity and no boundaries? How could I actually believe that I didn't have any value? How would I get out?

My husband and I operated a successful business for most of our eight years of marriage. We lived in a beautiful 110-year-old home that we restored together, situated in a neighborhood right out of a Norman Rockwell painting. We had a good life, frequently vacationing and traveling for business, and being able to afford whatever we needed. Sounds ideal, except that I was living a lie.

My big lie occurred the same way it does in many relationships. There were warning signs that I ignored early on. Like many women in their early 30's, I had a strong desire to get married, have a family and live the "dream." I knowingly ignored all of the precious messages. Consciously and subconsciously I relied on my own strength, stamina and competitiveness, as well as my belief that love can endure and cure anything. Those familiar attributes were slowly exhausted over the years until the Deanna I knew was sitting in a therapist's office, numb and checked out from reality, head down and hair covering her face.

My mother had recently passed, reminding me of the preciousness of life and creating a stir within me. Her death was the impetus for me to choose not to live in fear anymore. I wanted to live, and I knew I had to face the inevitable and make a plan for my escape with the children. The

amazing part of my story isn't that I left; it was the terrifying and paralyzing angst of that part of myself trying to convince me to stay when I woke up that Wednesday at 4:30 a.m. in a complete panic. Fear and doubt overwhelmed me; would I again give in and stay as I had done for way too long? Then all of a sudden, maternal warmth surrounded and soothed me like a soft blanket. In those moments, I knew I would be okay as long as I trusted the divine plan, remembered that I was doing the most loving thing for everyone involved.

"Thanks, Mom," I said quietly. That morning, the children and I fled our home with no glitches.

Within two days, I was served with papers from my spouse requesting joint custody of our two children. At motions court three weeks later, which my attorney advised me is customary to not attend, joint custody was awarded despite my attorney presenting page after page of allegations of domestic abuse. Just like that, I was essentially court ordered to only spend 50 percent of my time with my children, and if I didn't follow this decision, I would be in contempt of court.

I was emotionally crushed, devastated and bewildered that any judge would make such a decision despite claims of domestic violence. The following month, at the first of three conciliation hearings, normally held private among judge and attorneys as a routine check-in on domestic cases, I had a rare opportunity to meet the judge, sit in her chambers and interact. The judge specifically requested that my husband and I be present, and stated that no matter what happened during our marriage, we as parents needed to move forward and not be victims. I took her words to heart.

Meanwhile, I educated myself on all things divorce: laws, motions, verifications, assets and finances, discovery and other legal terminology. I read books written to help mothers

in the legal system, strongly suggesting that they look the part of "mother and victim" even while encouraging healing and self-empowerment. I attended parenting sessions and classes on the law that verged on offensive. The main message was to monitor and change my behavior so that the other party would be compliant. The system supposedly encourages family empowerment; however, the message I heard and was expected to heed was "remain a victim and stay quiet and everything will turn out nice on paper."

"I know that I have what it takes."

I worked on my own self-healing, to process all the hurt and fear. The wall that I kept banging my head against was the fight for sanity and affirmation in a system that doesn't recognize healing, empowerment and advocacy. Slowly, I found confidence in expressing my discontent and sharing my perception of my case with my attorney, the judge, and court counselors. I began to speak up for myself and my children. I had found my voice! A poem by Michelangelo Celli, Rejoice in Your Voice, came flooding back to me. I had a choice: I could play the blame game or speak from my compassionate self. I choose to advocate and speak.

After I left my marriage, I talked nonstop about the details to anyone who would listen. For two years, I "word vomited" all of my angst, sadness, grief, anger and fear onto my loving family, friends, therapists, attorneys, judge, even strangers. Sharing my story over and over was a part of my healing yet I realized that every time I delved into it, I experienced the trauma all over again. Even today, the memories of that difficult time remain with me, but my words are carefully chosen as I let go of the victim stance and focus on what I now create in my world.

So what does healing look like when we live in a social culture that wants to keep the victim victimized? I hired the best attorney money could buy, I had friends who patiently listened, and I had a support system that Oprah would admire. And I had my dedication to my own healing. I was now a single mother without a job. Being at this crossroad I chose to see this as an amazing opportunity to create a new life for my children and me. Now I could create a life with my own rules. I was excited yet terrified.

If you read my story with victim eyes you will get caught in the "power over" part in which I tell what happened; It might feel like: Oh poor me; it may appear that I am losing the battle. Or you can choose to read my story with an empowered perspective: I was not crushed by the system; I've stepped away from the system: I am currently cutting harmful entanglements and stepping onto a higher path in life and embracing the unknown.

My case is not yet over. There may be things during the divorce that not have turned out how I wanted it to; I didn't get everything that I wanted and felt I deserved. What I was able to achieve and I continue to focus on - which is extremely difficult and so undervalued - is a way being and a way of living to the fullest. I have developed patience and compassion. I look at my current situation with healing eyes. I expand my awareness and discernment every day so that I respond in the best interest of my family and not react with my emotions. I am building a better life for us and know that I have what it takes. I respect with a full heart of gratitude the divine influences in life. I am triumphant!

I don't listen to and believe the slew of words that are thrown my way and meant to devalue me. I don't look over my shoulder anymore. I am anchoring back into my body. I am able to co-parent with more patience and creativity. I

am free! My children and I live in a beautiful home that I created. I love myself and continue to heal. My hope is to help other families heal and move forward, as well. I have the compassion, patience and personal network that can benefit not only my own family but other families that need inspiration and hope. I live!

Deanna DiGioia is a devoted, compassionate mother and a certified holistic health coach. She helps individuals and families find their path to wellness through movement and nutrition. Deanna's passion is to encourage individuals and families stuck in the oppressive "power over" mindset to choose empowerment rather than victimhood. To learn more, go to chews-now.com

Brenda DeCroo

Your talents are divinely weaved together just for you to fulfill your purpose. What are you waiting for?"

\- Brenda DeCroo

Chapter Twenty-Five
A JOYFUL JOURNEY

Caught up in the whirlwind of a corporate career, I was on my way to the top. My days were filled with high demands, tight deadlines, and delivering valuable reports and analyses for making critical decisions. I put myself under pressure to be seen as the one who could get it all done. I wanted to be what I thought everyone wanted me to be. Inside I was dying, unsatisfied with the work and killing myself to get it done.

I wondered if it was possible to find the right/best/perfect job. I desperately wanted to be fulfilled in my work. I tried to be reassigned within the company to a position that aligned with my true values. My superiors were not willing to move me from one corporate function to another while I tried to find a place to fit in. I really enjoyed training and development. These were skills that came naturally to me and I got involved in it as much as I could. I mentored younger staff, guided managers in understanding their financial results and provided training in my area of expertise. I thought I had found my passion but the powers-that-be determined that accounting and finance is where I started and there I was to remain.

I'm not the type of woman who settles for taking up space and just coasting until retirement. If I wasn't able to express who I really am, use the gifts that God gave me and be joyful in my work, I wasn't going to waste any more precious time. I knew there had to be other options.

Frustrated, I recalled a career choice that I'd learned about years earlier. A friend and colleague with whom I often commiserated with about career dissatisfaction had told me about a new profession called coaching. It was a type of consulting that helped people to envision their goals, develop attainable plans, identify challenges and create the mindset for success and fulfillment. This appealed to me because deep listening, problem solving and helping others to be their best was something I had done since I was a child. Now with a renewed interest in coaching, I did some research and found that a local university was offering a six-month coaching program that fit perfectly into my schedule. Two months into it, I knew this was the work I wanted to do and felt confident that it would bring me joy and fulfillment.

To transition successfully, I had to eliminate the drain and distraction of the work that I hated, so I resigned from the security of my corporate job. My friends were so thrilled for me that they threw me a party. I suspected that they were living vicariously and saw me as making the same move they longed for in their hearts but were hesitant or afraid to follow. Even my boss admitted that he would love to escape the grind and have more time with his wife and young family. The CFO was impressed, telling me - and I quote - that he didn't think I had the balls to follow my dreams. It made me proud to know that I did, at least in the metaphorical sense!

I was off on my new adventure, starting my own business and creating the life of my dreams.

When we don't embrace who we are at the core and celebrate our greatest gifts, we're not fulfilling our purpose. The next time you recognize those feelings of not quite fitting in or not being good enough, but still longing to make a difference, ask yourself:

Am I on my true path?

Do I celebrate who I am?

Am I using my greatest gifts to make my highest contribution?

Making our highest contribution is the desire of every human being on this planet. Sadly, we often get too wrapped up in our fears and force ourselves to be what we believe we are "supposed" to be. This causes us to lose sight of what we love and what brings us joy, and prevents us from sharing our unique talents with the world.

"When we don't embrace who we are and celebrate our greatest gifts, we're not fulfilling our purpose."

Today I am a business and leadership coach working with others who are like I used to be: holding back from being the shining star they long to be. By helping my clients rediscover their core values and reclaim their strengths, I've found work that inspires me and allows me to live my purpose. Through coaching, I know that I'm making my highest contribution to the world. This makes my life much more joyful. When I am coaching clients, I encourage them to follow their hearts, face their challenges and keep moving forward. This is how they will create a life full of love and meaning.

Here are some of the strategies that I've applied and some lessons I've learned along the way:

Ask For Help

When I started my business, I felt as if my life's dream had come true. I was finally doing work that I loved. Being a business owner was more work than I had expected. All I wanted to do was coach people and help them solve their problems. I discovered that business owners have many additional responsibilities. Suddenly I found myself having to learn sales and marketing. I had no experience in these areas. I found myself having to step outside my comfort zone again and again.

Selling simply makes me uncomfortable. I worry about coming across as offensive and abrasive. This was a real challenge for me and I really struggled with it. In order to succeed in this business, I had to ask for help, and here's what I learned: Successful people love to help others be successful. Many of my new friends who had built their businesses and tackled the same challenges reached out to offer assistance. I accepted. Don't try to tough it out alone. Ask for what you need and your request will be answered.

Focus on Your Strengths

We all know there are certain things that just come natural to us. For me, it's my focus on relationships and my ability to envision the best for others. I instinctually seem to know what others can do to create their best outcomes and how to cheer them on to reach for their dreams. I've done this in my personal life for many years with family, friends and colleagues, and today with my coaching clients. I am known as the person who people can go to whenever they are facing a challenge and need to be heard, supported and

encouraged. Together, we excitedly map out plans to move forward to their continued success.

Get clear on what your strengths are and make sure that the biggest part of your life is spent doing things that make the most of your gifts. That's how you'll make your greatest contribution in the world.

Forgive Yourself

In my coaching practice we use an assessment called the Core Values Index (CVI). Through this assessment, I discovered a new personal awareness that removed a huge weight from my heart. For the many years that I had a successful corporate career, I was respected and well liked by my colleagues but I never really felt like I fulfilled my role to the satisfaction of the company's executives. When I became aware through CVI that these types of tasks are not aligned with my natural strengths and that I am actually demotivated by this is type of work, I felt such a relief. That's just not who I am; no wonder I felt a lack of gratification!

With this new realization, I finally let go of trying to be something I'm not. Forgiving myself for this self-judgment freed me to focus on the true gifts and talents that I bring to the world.

What disappointments are you holding on to? What have you not achieved in your life that is eclipsing all the good that you have accomplished? Get clear about what your true gifts are. Now, let those disappointments drift away. Forgive yourself and celebrate the beautiful, unique gifts you offer the world!

Create New Habits

Changing our circumstances is not a guarantee that we will change the way we act, think or be. Even though I left the corporate rat race, I still had a tendency to neglect taking care of myself. Setting out a schedule for exercise, meditation and healthy meals seemed like an easy plan, since these are all things that are important to me. But after a day or two, other tasks would infringe on these priorities. First one item, then the next item, and before I realized it, I was back to my neglectful habits. I finally realized that trying to change everything at the same time was setting myself up for failure.

It took some time but I learned to focus on adding just one new self-care practice at a time. Soon other healthy habits began to fall in place naturally. I've created long-lasting positive habits.

Are you looking to create new habits to make your life better in some way? Implement just one new habit today and then watch the effect it has on other areas of your life.

It took me a long time to find my place in the professional world. I learned that the path to anyplace worthwhile is never straight and level. I hope that sharing this story makes your journey a little easier by reminding you that you are not alone in your struggles. Remember to always embrace your gifts, as they are uniquely yours. Your talents are divinely weaved together just for you to fulfill your purpose. What are you waiting for?

Brenda DeCroo is an author, speaker and leadership coach. Using the Core Values Index, she helps managers and business owners create more profits. Brenda understands that when your employees are encouraged to use their unique talents, your company will enjoy increased productivity, less employee burnout and strong leadership development. Brenda earned her MBA from the University of Pittsburgh and is certified by the International Coach Federation. To learn how to get your own CVI assessment, visit TheAbundantBusiness.com.

"Your talents are divinely weaved together just for you to fulfill your purpose. What are you waiting for?"

- Brenda DeCroo

Here's to Your Inspired Life!

www.ingramcontent.com/pod-product-compliance
Lightning Source LLC
Chambersburg PA
CBHW052039090426
42739CB00010B/1973